THE THEOLOGY OF
WILLIAM BLAKE

THE THEOLOGY OF
WILLIAM BLAKE

BY

J. G. DAVIES

ARCHON BOOKS
1966

FIRST PUBLISHED 1948
THE CLARENDON PRESS

REPRINTED 1966 WITH PERMISSION OF
OXFORD UNIVERSITY PRESS
IN AN UNALTERED AND UNABRIDGED EDITION

LIBRARY OF CONGRESS CATALOG CARD NUMBER: 66-20229
PRINTED IN THE UNITED STATES OF AMERICA

PREFACE

IT has been said that to systematize Blake is to kill him. Whether or not I have been guilty of this crime is best left to the judgement of the reader, but in explanation of my object I should like to emphasize the obvious fact that no prose account of a poem can ever be taken as a substitute for the living verse. Yet such criticism and exposition may lead to a deeper understanding of what the poet has to say and therefore to a keener appreciation of his original utterance. If in some small measure I have achieved this, I shall have done all that I set out to do.

No student of Blake can fail to acknowledge his debt to Geoffrey Keynes, whose careful editing has so facilitated research. There have been numerous editions of Blake's writings, none of which agree on the line-numbering, owing to the fact that the order of the pages in his Prophetic books is frequently uncertain. I have therefore followed the standard one-volume edition by Geoffrey Keynes, first published in 1927, and I have reproduced Blake's irregular spelling and his peculiar use of capitals. I have deliberately given all the line references to Blake's works, and have carefully recorded my principal sources, for in pursuing my studies I found nothing more annoying than those many books about Blake which give not the slightest hint of the origin of their statements.

Of the many who have helped me in preparing this work I would like particularly to express my thanks to the Rev. Canon R. C. Mortimer who read the manuscript and made many useful suggestions, and also to the Rev. Canon L. Hodgson and Mr. H. M. Margoliouth, especially the latter, whose painstaking care was invaluable and who aided me to rectify numerous statements of error.

In conclusion I would acknowledge my gratitude to the Secretary and to the Delegates of the Clarendon Press, not only for accepting this work for publication but also for their patient assistance and expert guidance.

LONDON,   J. G. D.
October, 1947

CONTENTS

ABBREVIATIONS

Bacon.	Marginalia to Bacon's *Essays*, annotated *c.* 1798.
Berkeley.	Marginalia to Berkeley's *Siris*, annotated *c.* 1820.
Daughters of Albion.	*Visions of the Daughters of Albion.* 1793.
Laocoon.	The Laocoon group. 1820.
Last Judgment.	*Vision of the Last Judgment.* 1810.
Lavater.	Marginalia to Lavater's *Aphorisms*, annotated 1788.
M.D.L.W.	Marginalia to Swedenborg's *Divine Love and Wisdom*, annotated 1789.
M.D.P.	Marginalia to Swedenborg's *Divine Providence*, annotated 1790.
N.J.H.D.	Swedenborg's *The New Jerusalem and its Heavenly Doctrine.*
N.J.L.	Swedenborg's *Doctrine of the New Jerusalem concerning the Lord.*
N.J.S.	Swedenborg's *Doctrine of the New Jerusalem concerning the Scriptures.*
No Natural Religion.	*There is No Natural Religion.* 1788.
Reynolds.	Marginalia to Reynolds's *Discourses*, annotated *c.* 1808.
Thornton.	Marginalia to Thornton's *Translation of the Lord's Prayer*, annotated *c.* 1827.
Watson.	Marginalia to Watson's *Apology for the Bible*, annotated 1798.
Wordsworth.	Marginalia to Wordsworth's *Excursion*, annotated 1826.

I

INTRODUCTION

'I AM large, I contain multitudes', proclaimed Walt Whitman, defying in these words the narrowing logicality of circumscribed minds. The same declaration would have been equally fitting from the pen of William Blake, whose system of thought appears to include so many contrasting elements that the task of grasping it as a coherent whole seems wellnigh impossible. Yet a firm comprehension of his theology is indispensable if his works are to be fully understood and appreciated, for Blake, perhaps more than any other writer, was essentially a religious poet.

His critics are of little help in this respect, for few of them agree among themselves, and a collation of their estimates of his beliefs is bewildering in the extreme. Of his contemporaries, Benjamin Malkin, the writer of the first printed account of Blake, characterized him as a 'mystical philosopher' with 'enthusiastic and high-flown notions on the subject of religion'. Dr. Trusler, who in 1799 ordered from him a series of drawings which he later refused to accept, laconically scribbled on the artist's letter to him: 'Blake dim'd with superstition.' Frederick Tatham, to whom Catherine Blake bequeathed most of her husband's unpublished works, stoutly maintained that 'he was in all essential points orthodox in his belief'. Samuel Palmer, on the other hand, who knew Blake well, spoke of 'some of the doctrines in the poems, which seem to me to savour of Manicheism'; while Crabb Robinson, in his detailed, if uninspiring, autobiography, found it 'hard to fix Blake's station between Christianity, Platonism and Spinozism'. In more recent times the divergence of opinions is just as marked. To one, 'he might without great impropriety be numbered among those long-extinct sectaries the Marcionites';[1] to another, he was a 'heretic of the heresy of Swedenborg';[2] a third considers that 'he invented a heresy of the Holy Spirit, which, like an inverted

---

[1] *The Poetical Works of William Blake*, edited with a Prefatory Memoir by W. M. Rossetti, 1893, p. lxxxi.

[2] A. Symons, *William Blake*, 1907, p. 90.

B

Arian, he professed to be the whole Trinity in one';[1] a fourth, that he inherited many of the doctrines of Joachim of Flora.[2] In the opinion of some, he was a Gnostic; others return a verdict of pantheism. A more cautious group dismisses him as 'unorthodox'. While, finally, to complete the confusion, some critics affirm that he was after all a Christian, whose Christianity was 'orthodox in its main outlines'.

It is manifestly unscientific to place any writer or thinker in a specific religious category merely because one or more details of his teaching resemble those of some known heretic. To assume, for example, that, because a few sentences or paragraphs written by Blake can be paralleled in the systems of Basilides or Valentinus, he was therefore a Gnostic, is to take a superficial view of the problem and to neglect the complexities of his thought. Again, only one common feature is deemed necessary to herd Blake in with the British Israelites. It is true that Blake shared with the antiquaries of his age far-fetched notions of the origin of British civilization, which they traced back to the Druids and connected with the lost Ten Tribes; but Blake, while accepting such theories, was chiefly concerned in adapting them for symbolic purposes. Moreover, the British Israelites not only believe this unhistorical fantasy, but they also consider that military force is legitimate and necessary for the fulfilment of their mission; whereas Blake himself, after his earlier revolutionary enthusiasm had subsided, was a pacifist. Furthermore, the British Israelites interpret the Bible literally, at least such is their contention, while Blake always interpreted it according to its spiritual sense. Disregard of the obvious principle, that no individual should be classified as the member of a particular group or party unless he shares the majority of their essential tenets, has led to the further absurdity of some critics labelling Blake as an adherent of two different and separate heresies in one and the same book. One author can declare him a Gnostic and later a pantheist,[3] but these are two distinct heresies. Another can call him a Christian and follow this also by the statement that he was a pantheist, seemingly oblivious of the contradiction in which he has involved him-

[1] Osbert Burdett, *William Blake*, 1926, p. 191.
[2] G. K. Chesterton, *William Blake*, p. 156.
[3] R. Garnett, *William Blake, Poet and Painter*, 1895, pp. 30, 32.

self.[1] It is essential to take Blake as a whole, and not to think the quest for definition is ended when some doubtful similarity to a recognizable heresy has been discovered.

Blake himself was quite convinced that he had a message to proclaim: 'Mark well my words! they are of your eternal salvation',[2] he repeatedly warned his readers and urged them to make an effort to understand his doctrines, an effort which would bring its own reward.

> I give you the end of a golden string,
>   Only wind it into a ball,
> It will lead you in at Heaven's gate
>   Built in Jerusalem's wall.[3]

His friends and acquaintances were aware of the importance he attached to his beliefs, and a contemporary reviewer of his *Jerusalem* remarked that 'the doctor assures me that the redemption of mankind hangs on the universal diffusion of the doctrines broached in this MS.'. Although we must discount the rather sarcastic tone of this comment, it shows that Blake, at least, considered that he had produced a coherent system, thus fulfilling his declared object: 'I must Create a System, or be enslav'd by another Man's.'[4] Once having achieved this, he was not content to keep it to himself, and just as he drew Job recounting his experience to his daughters, showing them the way of salvation, so he attempted to spread his teaching among all who had ears to hear and eyes to read.

The object of this study is to attempt the elucidation of Blake's characteristic doctrines, which we have reason to believe lie embedded in his works, and then, on the basis of this outline, to define his religious position. The babel of conflicting opinions on this subject shows that such elucidation is not easy, despite Blake's belief to the contrary. 'I am happy', he wrote to Dr. Trusler, 'to find a Great Majority of Fellow Mortals who can Elucidate My Visions, & Particularly they have been Elucidated by Children.'[5] The existing confusion would seem to be due partly to Blake's own obscurity and the difficulty of interpreting his symbolism, and particularly to the fact that his critics have been neither children nor theologians but English

---

[1] C. Gardner, *Vision and Vesture*, 1929, pp. 174, 202.
[2] *Milton*, 2. 25.   [3] *Jerusalem*, 77.   [4] Ibid., 10. 20.
[5] 23 Aug. 1799.

scholars with their own sphere of appreciation, outside of which
they enter a realm comparatively unknown.

First, a brief consideration of the sources at our disposal is
necessary. The majority of Blake's writings have been preserved intact. Keynes, in his Bibliography, gives ten titles
which may represent works irrecoverably lost or still to be discovered, but in his judgement most of these were probably only
projected and never executed. The appearance of one or more
of these might lead to either greater clarity or further obscurity;
but whereas the possibility of such a discovery involves the
possibility that some conclusion might have to be altered, it
cannot be taken as sufficient grounds for refusing to consider the
material which is available, in an effort to appreciate the body
of Blake's doctrines. His system, as will be shown, is limited in
its scope, so that instead of covering ever-widening fields of
theological speculation Blake constantly reaffirmed the same
specific ideas; it follows that for any fresh discovery radically to
alter these central doctrines implies a revolution in Blake's
thought of which neither the details of his life nor the large
number of his writings which are extant give any suggestion.
Indeed, William Law's characterization of the works of Jacob
Boehme, one of Blake's masters and principal sources, is entirely
applicable to Blake himself: 'He (Boehme) always began again
afresh from the same first ground and full opening of the mystery
of nature, from whence he explained and determined the matter
he was upon. And it was this frequent and almost constant
repetition of one and the same ground that swelled his writings
into so many volumes, though it may be said that there is
nothing separately in any of his books but what is to be found in
almost every other, though not so largely set forth.' Similarly
in his conversation, Blake talked repeatedly of the same narrow
range of subjects, and so we find Crabb Robinson dismissing
some of his discussions with Blake as 'the same half crazy
crotchets about the two worlds', or the 'same round of extrava-
gant and mad doctrines'; 'it is', he wrote, 'so much a repetition
of his former talk.'

The rather obvious distinction of Blake's works into those
which were published and those which were not—the former
including poems, prophetical books, and prose writings, some
of them polemical, and the latter including further poems,

prophetic books, marginalia, letters, and epigrams—has been made the basis for the argument that only those works which were either printed or engraved can be taken as representative of Blake's mind; but this is by no means tenable. When Fuseli saw Blake's notes on Lavater he remarked, 'Any one could assuredly read your character in them', and this is equally true of his MS. book, which is a 'very intimate part of Blake'. Moreover, there is no reason to suppose that Blake ever intended his letters to be published, but no one can deny the right of his critics to use them as expressive of his mind and indicative of his ideas.

One factor, however, has constantly to be borne in mind when reading Blake's words, whether in his writings or in the reports of his life and conversation given by Gilchrist and Crabb Robinson, and that is his tendency to exaggeration, and arbitrariness when faced with stupidity or opposition. 'He retaliated', Tatham tells us, 'with such an eccentric answer as left the inquirer more afraid than ever. He then made an enigma of a plain question: hence arose many vague reports of his oddities. He was particularly so upon religion. His writings abound with these sallies of independent opinion . . . irritated by hypocrisy and the unequivocal yielding of weak and interested men, he said and wrote unwarrantable arguments.' This habit of giving vent to sarcasm which sometimes veiled his real opinion was freely admitted by Blake himself. 'Having spent the Vigour of my Youth & Genius under the Opression of Sr Joshua & his Gang of Cunning Hired Knaves Without Employment & as much as could possibly be Without Bread, The Reader must Expect to Read in all my Remarks on these Books Nothing but Indignation & Resentment.'[1] 'Resentment for Personal Injuries has had some share in this Public Address.'[2]

In his letters Blake seems consciously to have adopted 'a manner of speech intelligible to the recipients. He writes, for example, to Flaxman in a different language from that which he uses in his letters to Hayley and Butts.'[3] It was apparently his practice to make rough drafts of his letters and then send fair copies of them. If then, like St. Paul, Blake tried to be 'all

[1] Reynolds, fly-leaf.   [2] *Public Address*, p. 58.
[3] D. J. Sloss and J. P. R. Wallis, *The Prophetic Writings of William Blake*, 1926, vol. ii, p. 92.

things to all men', we have to be careful not to seize on seemingly orthodox phrases and immediately take them at their face
value when they may be nothing more than accommodations
to his correspondents' mental background.

In addition to all his writings, his paintings and engravings
are a most important source at our disposal. Blake is the only
man who has ever written, printed, and illustrated his own
books. His method of combining painting and poetry into one
complete whole is unique. He turned 'almost indifferently from
the one to the other as a means of expressing exact ideas'.[1] This
fact supplies the explanation of his remark to Crabb Robinson
that the absurd diagrams in the Law edition of Jacob Boehme
were equal to the works of Michelangelo. His meaning was
that the conception behind them was as great as the conceptions
of Michelangelo. Sometimes the drawings and engravings are
simply straightforward illustrations of the words; sometimes
they develop a different but parallel theme, giving a contra-
puntal effect; most frequently they are so part of the text that
the one cannot be understood without the other. Blake then
used his painting equally with his poetry and prose to convey
his message. 'Blake's art indeed', wrote Roger Fry, 'is a test case
for our theories of aesthetics. It boldly makes the plea for art
that it is a language for conveying impassioned thought and
feeling, which takes up the objects of sense as a means to this
end, owing them no allegiance and accepting from them only
the service they can render for this purpose.' In seeking to
interpret his designs we need not, however, look for a symbolism of colour, despite Messrs. Ellis and Yeats's declaration to
the contrary, since he illuminated separate copies of the same
work differently.

With this material before us, we can now attempt to outline
Blake's theological ideas. We may expect to find some apparent
contradictions in the work of a man who could declare that
'Without Contraries is no progression';[2] if such paradoxes are
encountered we can but state them plainly and hint at a possible
reconciliation in that Unity towards which, according to Blake,
the multiplicity of existence is constantly being drawn. Again,
we must expect some development of doctrine, for he despised

---

[1] J. Wicksteed, *Blake's Innocence and Experience*, 1928, p. 25.
[2] *Marriage of Heaven and Hell*, p. 3.

the mind which, hesitating to go forward, stagnates in its own conservatism. 'The man who never alters his opinion is like standing water, & breeds reptiles of the mind',[1] therefore 'expect poison from the standing water'.[2]

First we shall seek to understand his attitude and relation to the Church; this will lead us on to a discussion of the extent to which he was indebted to Swedenborg, and thence to the core of his personal religion, his mysticism; finally the various elements of his system will present themselves for detailed consideration.

[1] Ibid., p. 19.   [2] Ibid., p. 9.

II

BLAKE AND THE CHURCH

WILLIAM BLAKE was born on the 28th of November 1757, and was baptized on the 11th of December from the Grinling Gibbon's font in the Wren Church, St. James's, Westminster. He was married to Catherine Boucher in the newly rebuilt parish church of Battersea, on Sunday, 18 August 1782. At his own wish he was buried according to the rites and ceremonies of the Church of England in Bunhill Fields, on Friday, 17 August 1827. These are the only known occasions, in a life of nearly seventy years, on which Blake took part in the services of the Established Church. As a boy, his apprenticeship to the engraver Basire had led him to make drawings from the monuments in Westminster Abbey, but during the services the vergers turned the key on him. There is, in fact, no evidence, other than the three bare facts already listed, that he ever went to church, and indeed, J. T. Smith, a contemporary and acquaintance of Blake, wrote in 1828: 'I admit he did not for the last forty years attend any place of Divine worship.'

The reason for Blake's failure to be a practising Churchman was twofold. In the first place, he adhered strictly to Christ's injunction: 'when thou prayest, enter into thine inner chamber, and having shut the door, pray to thy Father which is in secret'; 'I have endeavoured to live as Christ commands,' he said on his death-bed, 'and have sought to worship God truly—in my own house, when I was not seen of men.' In the second place, he was fiercely antagonistic to the Church itself. 'The Modern Church Crucifies Christ with the Head Downwards',[1] this biting phrase, echoing the legend of St. Peter's martyrdom, known to Blake from Michelangelo's painting, sets the note of Blake's criticism of the Church as it existed in his day, and indeed the quality of its devotion and the character of its leaders left much to be desired.

The general condition of religious life in eighteenth-century England, as it must have presented itself to Blake, may be con-

[1] *Last Judgment*, p. 87.

veniently summarized in these words of William Law: 'we live starving in the coldness and deadness of a formal, historical, hearsay-religion . . . we keep all things quiet within us, partly by outward forms and modes of religion and morality, and partly by the comforts, cares and delights of this world.' For confirmation of the latter part of this statement we may turn to Hartley, who in his *Observations on Man* (1749) listed six evils likely to lead to the dissolution of 'the present States of Christendom', and his fifth item is the 'gross neglect of duty by the worldly-minded clergy'. The worldly-mindedness of the bishops was evident to all, and one of their number, Richard Watson, Bishop of Llandaff, complained of the spectacle of 'the generality of bishops bartering their independence and the dignity of their order for the chance of a translation, and polluting gospel-humility by the pride of prelacy'. Nepotism, sinecures, pluralities, and non-residence were rife. Herring, for instance, held the deanery of Rochester *in commendam* with the bishopric of Bangor; Wilcocks was Bishop of Rochester and Dean of Westminster; Hoadley held the see of Bangor for six years, and during the whole of that time was never once in his diocese. Most bishops spent eight or nine months of the year in London and only the remaining three or four months in their dioceses.

It is not surprising therefore to find that the clergy stood aloof from the people, for spending so much time and energy in promoting their own interests, they took little notice of the miserable plight of the majority of the population, and those few priests who did so only threw into greater relief the apathy of the Church as a whole. The Church's disregard of social problems disgusted Blake, who saw

> How the Chimney-sweeper's cry
> Every black'ning Church appalls;[1]

and her lack of sympathy with the physical needs of mankind received satiric condemnation in his 'Little Vagabond'.

Blake's antagonism to the Church was further increased by the political subservience of the bishops, who without scruple played a prominent part in parliamentary elections, using their influence and position to obtain support for their party, an

---

[1] 'London', stanza 3.

activity which elicited Dr. Johnson's famous remark: 'No man
can now be made a bishop for his learning and piety; his only
chance of promotion is his being connected with someone who
has parliamentary interest.' This did mean, however, that
there was a most harmonious association of Church and State,
but no one could maintain that it was an edifying spectacle. It
was against this that Blake mainly directed his marginal com-
ments in his copy of Bishop Watson's *Apology*. 'The Beast & the
Whore rule without control', he declared on the back of the
title-page, referring to the State and the Church. 'State Religion . . . is the source of all Cruelty' (p. 25). 'To what does the
Bishop attribute the English Crusade against France? Is it not
to State Religion? Blush for shame' (p. 2). Blake believed him
to be writing in the pay of the Government, 'I believe him to
be a State trickster' (p. 1). This was most unfair to Watson
who was left in the see of Llandaff from 1782 to 1819 because he
opposed the supporters of the American war and was pre-
eminent for his political independence; still, Watson and
Jonathan Shipley, who for the same reason remained Bishop of
St. Asaph from 1769 till his death there in 1788, were excep-
tions, and to Blake the political allegiance of the episcopal
bench as a whole was the greatest of blasphemies; it was to
worship Caesar and not our Lord.

If the episcopacy inspired Blake with little respect, there was
even less reason for him to be attracted to the lower clergy,
between whom and the bishops there was a great gulf, the
former being for the most part in penury and abject poverty.
Preferment was easy for the minority of noble birth, but for
those with no influence and with no private sources of income
it was all but impossible, and even their actual admission to the
ranks of the clergy was delayed and prolonged beyond measure.
so that many curates never advanced beyond the diaconate.
Archdeacon Blackburne, writing in 1754, spoke of the body of
clergy 'whose lives and occupations are most foreign to their pro-
fessions', and of 'the ignorant herd of poor curates'. In their
quest for the wherewithal to keep body and soul together, the
clergy earned the reputation of being rapacious, hence Blake's
reference to 'the Priest's o'ergorged Abdomen',[1] and his caustic
epigram:

[1] *Vala*, 9. 246.

'Why of the sheep do you not learn peace?'
'Because I don't want you to shear my fleece.'

The priest cursed the earth instead of blessing it, and 'in deadly black' devoured its labour. Blake himself was so little attached to the things of this world—he did not 'value such things as these'[1]—that to see the clergy devoting so much of their time to monetary matters was enough to condemn them in his eyes as materialists and utter strangers to the realms of the spirit:

> With what sense does the parson claim the labour of the farmer?
> What are his nets & gins & traps; & how does he surround him
> With cold floods of abstraction, and with forests of solitude,
> To build him castles and high spires, where kings & priests may dwell.[2]

His repugnance for the Church was further increased by her attitude to art. The man to whom 'Christianity is Art',[3] to whom 'Jesus & his Apostles & Disciples were all Artists',[3] and to whom 'The Mocker of Art is the Mocker of Jesus',[4] could have had little patience with a Church which seemed to go out of its way to neglect the works of painters. Cathedrals were ill used and ill kept; the usual method of decoration was white-wash, and any suggestion of further adornment was condemned as popery. The general sentiment of the age was against mural paintings and altar-pieces, as Bishop Newton, in his capacity as Dean of St. Paul's, discovered, when Bishop Terrick of London vetoed the proposal made by Sir Joshua Reynolds and a company of artists to paint sacred pictures around the dome of the cathedral. No wonder that Blake should have complained bitterly 'The Painters of England are unemploy'd in Public works. . . . Painting is excluded. Painting, the Principal Art, has no place amongst our almost only public works.'[5] It was in vain, therefore, and no doubt with a sense of frustration, that he executed drawings to be done 'in Fresco on an enlarged scale to ornament the altars of churches'.[6]

But if the Church's neglect of the arts annoyed him, her attitude to morals only served to infuriate him further. The

[1] 'I rose up at the dawn of day.'   [2] *Daughters of Albion*, 128–31.
[3] Laocoon.   [4] *To Hayley*, 11 Dec. 1805.
[5] *Public Address*, p. 23.   [6] *Descriptive Catalogue*, xiv.

Anglican clergy took Tillotson as their model throughout the eighteenth century, some of them, such as James Woodforde (1740–1803), frequently reproducing the *ipsissima verba*. The popularity of Tillotson's sermons is a most important factor in understanding the piety of the period, which was 'perhaps above all, a piety that had digested Revelation into Reason, and consequently took little interest in Christian Doctrine, except as a support for Christian Ethics'.[1] This emphasis on reason and conduct was the product of Latitudinarianism, resulting in a profound distrust of fanaticism and enthusiasm. One Georgian bishop was praised on his tombstone for his zeal in repressing enthusiasm; while in proposing the health of the newly consecrated first Bishop of Calcutta, the Archbishop of Canterbury (Manners Sutton) said: 'Remember, my Lord Bishop, that your Primate on the day of your consecration defined your duty for you:—that duty is to put down enthusiasm and preach the Gospel.' The enthusiasm thus deprecated was not enthusiasm in the sense in which it is used to-day, as a zeal or earnest feeling, nor was it synonymous with fanaticism; but it may be defined as 'a misconceit of inspiration'. 'It thus became a sort of byeword, applied in opprobrium and derision to all who laid claim to a spiritual power or divine guidance, such as appeared to the person by whom the term of reproach was used, fanatical extravagance, or, at the least, an unauthorised outstepping of all rightful bounds of reason.'[2] This was anathema to Blake, who believed he was 'under the direction of Messengers from Heaven, Daily & Nightly'.[3]

The way rationalism had established itself in the Church, a considerable time before Blake's birth, is illustrated by the action of Bishop Burnet, who died in 1715, in finding fault with the Creator for the disorder of the stars in the heavens. 'What a beautiful hemisphere they would have made if they had been placed in rank and order; if they had all been disposed in regular figures; the little ones set with due regard to the greater, and then all finished and made up into one fair piece, or great composition, according to the rules of art and symmetry.' This was the Age of Reason with Deism as one of the foremost factors

[1] C. Smyth, *The Art of Preaching, 747–1939*, 1940, p. 158.
[2] C. J. Abbey and J. H. Overton, *The English Church in the Eighteenth Century*, 1902, p. 227.　　　　[3] *To Butts*, 10 Jan. 1802.

in religious life, and reason itself the yard-stick by means of which the credibility of anything and everything was estimated. It culminated in the enthronement of the goddess Reason by the fanatics of the French Revolution. This over-emphasis of reason, to the exclusion of the other equally important elements in man's mental and spiritual make-up, led, in Blake's view, to a far too narrow conception of the nature of man and God; the heart and soul were divorced from the mind. Eighteenth-century man, in fact, was imprisoned in 'Mind-forg'd manacles';[1] his capacity for further knowledge was inhibited, for 'Man by his reasoning power can only compare & judge of what he has already perciev'd'.[2] Hence Blake's implacable antagonism to reason, which he personified in his mythology as the character Urizen, 'cold & scientific'.[3]

Although Blake believed that reason might be redeemed ultimately and restored to its rightful place in man's psychology, he resisted its tyranny, and in so doing went to the extreme of even denying its validity. 'Downright Plain Truth is Something, But Reasoning is Nothing.'[4] Reason, he asserted to Crabb Robinson, is 'the creature of man and opposed to God's grace'. 'Away with your reasoning', he said, 'and your rubbish',[5] and declared 'I will not Reason & Compare: my business is to Create'.[6] He condemned reason in the first instance because it undermines inspiration:

The idiot Reasoner laughs at the Man of Imagination,
And from laughter proceeds to murder by undervaluing calumny.[7]

He considered that rational analysis takes away the very life from the object analysed, it is indeed tantamount to murder. So in his poem 'Infant Joy' he said that joy has no name, because 'its very being is lost in the great tide of selfless delight',[8] and so to examine it, to classify it, to analyse it, is to destroy it:

Why wilt thou Examine every little fibre of my soul,
Spreading them out before the sun like stalks of flax to dry?
The infant joy is beautiful, but its anatomy
Horrible, Ghast & Deadly.[9]

[1] 'London', stanza 2.   [2] No Natural Religion, I. II.   [3] Jerusalem, 43. 2.
[4] Watson, p. 29.   [5] Descriptive Catalogue, v.   [6] Jerusalem, 10. 21.
[7] Milton, 35. 6, 7.   [8] E. Underhill, The Fruits of the Spirit, 1942, p. 15.
[9] Vala, I. 43–6.

Blake had no sympathy with the mentality that always seeks for proof:

> He's a Blockhead who wants a proof of what he can't Percieve
> And he's a Fool who tries to make such a Blockhead believe.[1]

Nor could he see the possibility of discovering new truths by the scientific method of experiment, which he realized was unable to give any explanation of the phenomena observed, being incapable of discovering meaning, and giving only descriptions in mathematical terms.[2]

> As to that false appearance which appears to the reasoner
> As of a Globe rolling thro' Voidness, it is a delusion of Ulro.
> The Microscope knows not of this nor the Telescope: they alter
> The ratio of the Spectator's Organs, but leave Objects untouch'd.[3]

So he wanted 'the intire abrogation of Experimental Theory',[4] 'to cast off Rational Demonstration by Faith in the Saviour'.[5]

> To cast off the idiot Questioner who is always questioning
> But never capable of answering;[6]

and he commented sarcastically in a fragment of verse:

> 'Doubt, Doubt, & don't believe without experiment':
> That is the very thing that Jesus meant,
> When he said, 'Only Believe! Believe & try!
> 'Try, Try, and never mind the Reason why.'

Faith itself will prove the fact, in so far as it can be proved; reality is 'of Faith & not of Demonstration'.[7] Blake agreed with Whitman that 'wisdom is of the Soul, is not susceptible of proof, is its own proof'.

It was reason which Blake took to be at the root of the preoccupation with morality and the consequent neglect of the well-springs of religious devotion. 'Our judgment of right & wrong is Reason.'[8] Reason

> when separated
> From Imagination and closing itself as in steel in a Ratio
> Of the things of Memory, It thence frames Laws & Moralities
> To destroy Imagination, the Divine Body, by Martyrdoms & Wars.[9]

---

[1] Epigram.
[2] This opinion of Blake's is identical with that of Sir James Jeans; cf. *Physics and Philosophy*, 1943, pp. 15, 16.   [3] *Milton*, 31. 15-18.
[4] *Jerusalem*, 52.   [5] *Milton*, 48. 3.   [6] Ibid., 48. 12, 13.
[7] *Jerusalem*, 31. 46.   [8] Watson, p. 2.   [9] *Jerusalem*, 74. 10-13.

This reveals a clear understanding of the circumstances, for reason had undermined the supernatural with the consequent supersession of religion by ethics.

The outcome of this attitude to reason and enthusiasm was that the sermon became a moral essay, whose subject was utilitarian ethics. That some of the dignitaries of the Church were not unaware of this fact is evidenced by the words of Archdeacon Paley, in his Charge to the clergy of the Diocese of Carlisle in 1790: 'we are . . . setting up a kind of philosophical morality, detached from religion and independent of its influence.' In the same year Bishop Horsley, in his Charge to the clergy of the Diocese of St. David's, condemned 'another maxim, which I never hear without extreme concern from the lips of a divine, either from the pulpit or in familiar conversation—namely, that practical religion and morality are one and the same thing—that moral duties constitute the whole or by far the better part of practical Christianity'; but 'I flatter myself that we are in a state of recovery from this delusion. The compositions which are at this day delivered from our pulpits are, I think, in general of a more Christian cast than were often heard some thirty years since, when I first entered on the ministry.' But the Bishop of St. David's was too optimistic, for in 1826 Hugh James Rose, delivering his course on *The Commission and Consequent Duties of the Clergy*, opened his argument with a quotation from a sermon preached by Tillotson before the House of Commons on 5 November 1678: 'For God's sake, what is Religion good for, but to reform the Manners and Dispositions of Men, to restrain human Nature from Violence and Cruelty, from Falshood and Treachery, from Sedition and Rebellion?' and continued:

Its utility in this view is perhaps condescendingly recognized, and even that of a ministry sometimes acknowledged, as being a body of men whose business it is to enforce the obligations to good order and moral duty, and to terrify those who might hope to evade human laws, by holding up to their imagination and their fears an invisible power, and a future retribution. But any belief that God has himself instituted certain means, through the medium of which he confers internal and spiritual grace, any belief that through these means he seeks to open that communion with his creatures without which the high gifts of reason, of genius, of the soul itself, if not as worthless and

as dead as this fair bodily frame when the spark of life is gone, yet
subsist in a low and degraded state, any such belief, I fear, exists not,
in the present day, with any large portion of mankind.[1]

The laity as a whole seldom worshipped God, but, in the
words of Archbishop Secker, 'flattered themselves that what
they are pleased to call a moral and harmless life, though far
from being either, is the one thing needful'. This was sympto-
matic of the spiritual decadence of the age, for moralistic appeals
indicate a loss of religious vitality.

The predominant theme of sermons being such, Blake looked
upon 'Clergymen in the Pulpit' as 'scourging Sin instead of
Forgiving it';[2] priests were nothing but inquisitors,[3] they were
the agents of repression,[4] the cursers of innocent joys.[5] 'As the
caterpillar chooses the fairest leaves to lay her eggs on, so the
priest lays his curse on the fairest joys.'[6]

> And the gates of this Chapel were shut,
> And 'Thou shalt not' writ over the door;
>
> .   .   .   .
>
> And Priests in black gowns were walking their rounds,
> And binding with briars my joys & desires.[7]

The Church was lacking in compassion and forgiveness: 'Wo,
Wo, Wo, to you Hypocrites. Even Murder, the Courts of
Justice, more merciful than the Church, are compell'd to allow
is not done in Passion, but in Cool Blooded design & Inten-
tion.'[8]

> Thy purpose & the purpose of thy Priests & of thy Churches
> Is to impress on men the fear of death, to teach
> Trembling & fear, terror, constriction, abject selfishness.[9]

All that the Church did was to preach stern duty, passive
obedience to the 'stony law',[10] which issues in 'the tears &
sighs & death sweat of the Victims',[11] but this is to worship the
'God of this world', Satan and not Jesus, for 'if Morality was

---

[1] This and the preceding quotations are taken from Smyth, op. cit.
[2] *Last Judgment*, pp. 76–7. [3] Watson, p. 1.
[4] 'A Little Boy Lost.' [5] *French Revolution*, 225.
[6] *Marriage of Heaven and Hell*, p. 9. [7] 'The Garden of Love.'
[8] *Last Judgment*, p. 87. [9] *Milton*, 43. 37–9.
[10] 'Song of Liberty', 20. [11] *Vala*, 8. 226.

Christianity, Socrates was the Saviour'.[1] Indeed, this emphasis upon the observance of the moral code, which seemed just as rigidly enforced as the ancient Jewish adherence to the torah, produced dire effects in the life of the community, for 'Prisons are built with stones of Law, Brothels with bricks of Religion'.[2] So it was that Blake rejected the Church as 'cruel',[3] as making 'up a heaven of our misery',[4] and as hypocritical because abstinence was preached but not practised.[5] The Church, so far from preaching the Gospel, was, if anything, conducting a 'Most Malignant & Artful attack upon the Kingdom of Jesus'.[6] The beliefs propagated by ecclesiastics, according to Blake, are to be found in his translation of Dr. Thornton's translation of the Lord's Prayer:

Our Father Augustus Ceasar, who art in these thy Substantial Astronomical Telescopic Heavens, Holiness to thy Name or Title, & reverence to thy Shadow. Thy Kingship come upon Earth first & then in Heaven. Give us day by day our Real Taxed Substantial Money bought Bread; deliver from the Holy Ghost whatever cannot be Taxed; for all is debts & Taxes between Caesar & us & one another; lead us not to read the Bible, but let our Bible be Virgil & Shakespeare; & deliver us from Poverty in Jesus, that Evil One. For thine is the Kingship, [or] Allegoric Godship, & the Power, or War, & the Glory, or Law, Ages after Ages in thy descendants; for God is only an Allegory of Kings & nothing Else.

Amen.[7]

As long as one had no difficulties to face, the Christianity of the Church was no doubt acceptable and pleasant, or at least inoffensive, and belief in a beneficent providence was quite congenial, but the moment one encountered any problem or met with misery and despair, the Church was utterly incapable of giving help, so that suffering humanity was left 'pining in bonds of religion'.[8]

It is an easy thing to triumph in the summer's sun
And in the vintage & to sing on the waggon loaded with corn.
It is an easy thing to talk of patience to the afflicted,
To speak the laws of prudence to the houseless wanderer,

---

[1] Laocoon.
[2] *Marriage of Heaven and Hell*, p. 8.
[3] *Last Judgment*, pp. 76–7.
[4] 'The Chimney Sweeper', stanza 3.
[5] *America*, 128.
[6] Thornton, title-page.
[7] Ibid., fly-leaf.
[8] *America*, 200.

To listen to the hungry raven's cry in wintry season
When the red blood is fill'd with wine & with the marrow of
    lambs.
It is an easy thing to laugh at wrathful elements,
To hear the dog howl at the wintry door, the ox in the
    slaughter house moan;
To see a god on every wind & a blessing on every blast;
To hear sounds of love in the thunder storm that destroys
    our enemies' house;
To rejoice in the blight that covers his field, & the sickness that
    cuts off his children,
While our olive & vine sing & laugh round our door, & our
    children bring fruits & flowers.
Then the groan & the dolor are quite forgotten, & the slave
    grinding at the mill,
And the captive in chains, & the poor in the prison, & the
    soldier in the field
When the shatter'd bone hath laid him groaning among the
    happier dead.
It is an easy thing to rejoice in the tents of prosperity,[1]

but in adversity, Blake believed, the Church could give no
succour, and he looked forward to a time when the shackles of
sacerdotalism should be burst asunder:

Let the slave, grinding at the mill, run out into the field;
Let him look up into the heavens & laugh in the bright air.
Let the inchained soul, shut up in darkness & in sighing,
Whose face has never seen a smile in thirty weary years,
Rise & look out: his chains are loose, his dungeon doors are
    open;
And let his wife & children return from the opressor's scourge.

They look behind at every step & believe it is a dream.
Are these the slaves that groan'd along the streets of Mystery?
Where are your bonds & task masters? are these the prisoners?
Where are your chains? where are your tears? why do you
    look around?
If you are thirsty, there is the river: go, bathe your parched
    limbs,
The good of all the Land is before you, for Mystery is no
    more.[2]

[1] *Vala*, 2. 405–20.   [2] Ibid., 9. 668–79.

Yet Blake's rejection of the Church was not entirely due to the decadent state in which he found it, nor to the false emphasis in its teaching; he was also opposed on principle to the ecclesiastical ideal of public worship; he did not see the need of it. 'Every man may converse with God & be a King & Priest in his own house.'[1] William Law speaks of the soul as the 'Temple of God within thee . . . where alone thou canst worship God in spirit and in truth. . . . When once thou art well grounded in this inward worship, thou wilt have learnt to live unto God above time and place. For every day will be Sunday to thee, and wherever thou goest thou wilt have a priest, a church, and an altar along with thee.' This conception is one found frequently in the works of the mystics, and Blake under the influence of such views, carrying them to their logical conclusion, denied the necessity of corporate worship. In like manner Wesley interpreted this passage of Law's as meaning that there is no need to attend church, but Law himself was a regular communicant, and similar expressions are to be found, e.g. in the sermons of Tauler, who was at the same time a monk and an ecclesiastic. Blake was unable to hold these two elements, of private devotion and corporate worship, in the tension achieved by orthodoxy; for him to work was to pray: 'The Whole of the New Church is in the Active Life & not in Ceremonies at all',[2] and 'The outward Ceremony is Antichrist'.[3] He could perceive no causal connexion between churchgoing and good deeds, in fact worshippers seemed worse rather than better than other folk, and Blake could not tolerate the religious energy which expended itself in devotion and had no time for human needs, as in the case of the chimney-sweep's father and mother, who left him freezing in the snow and 'are both gone up to the church to pray'.[4] Moreover, as Blake considered matter to be frequently an impediment to the apprehension of reality, and too great an emphasis on it as leading to the denial of the spiritual, he rejected all outward ceremony; in fact 'the Worship of God' is nothing more nor less than 'honouring his gifts in other men & loving the greatest men

[1] Watson, pp. 8–9.
[2] M.D.L.W., p. 181.
[3] Laocoon.
[4] 'The Chimney Sweeper.'

best'.[1] It follows that any form of sacramentalism was meaning-
less to him:

> overthrow their cup,
> Their bread, their altar-table, their incense and their oath,
> Their marriage & their baptism, their burial & consecration.[2]

He did, on occasion, speak of the Eucharist and Baptism in
words which seem to appraise them highly, but his use of the
terms was entirely symbolic. In describing his picture of the
Last Judgement, he said, of the apostles standing one on each
side of heaven, 'that on the Right Represents Baptism, that on
the Left Represents the Lord's Supper. All Life consists of these
Two, Throwing off Error & Knaves from our company continually & Recieving Truth or Wise Men into our Company
continually.'[3] Thus his vision of Baptism and the Eucharist in
heaven does not mean that he accepted them: he was merely
using them as symbols to suggest the casting off of error and the
reception of truth. To him the Eucharist was always a symbol,
and never a sacrament, e.g.

> And My Brother is there, & My Friend & Thine
> Descend & ascend with the Bread & the Wine.
> The Bread of sweet Thought & the Wine of Delight.[4]

This emphasis on the active life meant that Blake had little
good to say of the Church of his day; indeed one of his few kind
remarks, if not the only one, referred to a charitable institution
set up by the Church, namely, St. Thomas's Hospital, which is
'one of the most amiable features of the Christian Church'.[5]

The spiritual decadence of the Church, her preoccupation
with questions of finance and political jobbery, her attitude to
reason and enthusiasm, to morals and art, the whole of her
sacramental system and her neglect of social problems, so
affected Blake that he conceived a lifelong hatred for the priest-
hood. The clergy of his day were the contemporary Pharisees,
who 'bind heavy burdens and grievous to be borne, and lay

---

[1] *Jerusalem*, 91. 7, 8.   [2] Ibid., 91. 12–14.
[3] *Last Judgment*, pp. 82–4.   [4] *To Mrs. Flaxman*, 14 Sept. 1800.
[5] *Prospectus of the Engraving of Chaucer's Canterbury Pilgrims*. Yet even here it is
doubtful whether Blake gave his unqualified approval, because he objected to
organized charity on the grounds that it left no room for personal sympathy:
'pity is become a trade, and generosity a science That men get rich by' (*America*,
124, 125).

them on men's shoulders', who 'shut the kingdom of heaven against men', they are 'hypocrites', 'whited sepulchres', 'serpents' and 'offspring of vipers'. 'Read the xxiii Chap. of Matthew & then condemn Paine's hatred of Priests if you dare.'[1] Such was Blake's dislike of them that when Sir Joshua Reynolds, in his *Discourses*, referred incidentally to someone who had originally been a Dissenting Minister, Blake's brief comment was 'Villainy!' (p. xxxiv).

Nevertheless, despite his vigorous denunciation of all that was evil in the Church of his day, 'Blake escaped the wholesale condemnation of Christianity to which Paine and Shelley succumbed. Instead it is one of the greatest proofs of his intellectual clarity that Blake could distinguish so definitely between the Churches and the religion of Christ',[2] because he saw that all forms of organized religion, however impregnated with error, still preserve a portion of truth, and he was not one of those illogical persons who immediately condemn a doctrine because he who teaches it does not practise what he preaches.

His theological conception of the Church, so far as it can be gathered from very scant references, has several affinities with orthodox doctrine. He saw quite correctly that the Church descends from and in a sense continues the congregation of the children of Israel; 'The Christian Church, who are the Offspring of the Hebrew.'[3] The Church is under divine guidance and protection, which she does not forfeit even when infected with radical evil: 'the Latter state of the Church when on the verge of Perdition, yet protected by a Flaming Sword.'[4] Salvation is mediated through the Church, but this does not necessarily exclude those who are without; he implied this when he said: 'these represent those who were not in the Line of the Church & yet were Saved from among the Antediluvians who Perished.'[4] He was careful to stress the point that to be outside the Church does not by any means involve being outside the sphere of redemption, and thereby he defended his own position: 'He who is out of the Church & opposes it is no less an Agent of Religion than he who is in it.'[4] 'That the Jews assumed a right Exclusively to the benefits of God will be a

---

[1] Watson, opp. list of books.
[2] Allardyce Nicholl, *William Blake and His Poetry*, 1922, p. 63.
[3] *Last Judgment*, pp. 80-1.   [4] Ibid., pp. 82-4.

lasting witness against them & the same will it be against
Christians.'[1] Blake tended also to maintain a distinction
between the visible and the invisible Church: 'the Church
Universal ... There is such a State in Eternity: it is composed of
the Innocent civilized Heathen & the Uncivilized Savage who,
having not the Law, do by Nature the things contain'd in the
Law.'[2] This idea of the invisible Church as the body of true
believers, to be distinguished from the visible Church, which
contains both true and untrue Christians, has no basis in
Scripture and is absent from pre-Reformation teaching; it is
in part a means to discredit the visible Church. Blake did not
discuss the relationship of Christ to the Church, although he
said, without specific application, that each one of us is a
'Divine Member of the Divine Jesus';[3] nor did he mention the
activity of the Holy Spirit in the Church. We can only conclude
from this either that he attached no importance to such
questions or that he did not hold any beliefs about them, for
in Blake's case the argument *e silentio* is nearly always valid,
because he was so concerned about the 'minute particulars', so
careful to present everything in its entirety, that any omission
indicates that what is omitted was either irrelevant or of no
great value in his eyes.

> He who wishes to see a Vision, a perfect Whole,
> Must see it in its Minute Particulars.[4]

Inseparable in Blake's mind from his opposition to the
Church was his aversion to the Deists, whose ideas the Church
successfully combated, but a considerable number of which she
unconsciously absorbed.

The first mention of the Deists comes in a work by the French-
man Viret, *Instruction chrétienne*, published in 1563, but it was
not until the following century that any one of note was to be
found in their ranks. In 1624 Lord Herbert of Cherbury
published his *De Veritate* to be followed much later by his *De
Religione Gentilium* in 1663. The actual beginning of the Deist
controversy was occasioned, however, by the appearance, in
1695, of John Locke's *The Reasonableness of Christianity*. His main
thesis was that 'Reason is natural revelation whereby the eternal

[1] Watson, pp. 7–8.   [2] *Last Judgment*, pp. 80–1.
[3] *Jerusalem*, 91. 30.   [4] Ibid., 91. 20–1.

Father of light and fountain of all knowledge communicates to mankind that portion of truth which he has laid within the reach of their natural faculties: revelation is natural reason enlarged by a new set of discoveries communicated by God immediately, which reason vouchsafes the truth of, by the testimony and proofs it gives, that they came from God.' He was thus the advocate of what may be called a 'supernatural rationalism'. His aim, as evidenced by the title, was to demonstrate the reasonableness of Christianity; but this opened the way to accepting some parts of the Gospel as reasonable and rejecting others as unreasonable. This further step was taken by Toland, Locke's young Irish disciple, in his *Christianity not Mysterious*, which was issued the following year (1696).

The next stage in the development of the Deist case took place in 1730, when Matthew Tindal's *Christianity as Old as Creation* appeared, a work which earned the title of the 'Deist's Bible'. Tindal affirmed that everything genuine in Christianity is derived from natural religion and has existed from the Creation; human nature is unchangeable and the moral code is static and identical with 'natural law'. Thus Deism had reached a frankly antichristian position, for according to their reasoning the revelation of God through His Son was superfluous.

Briefly their main tenets were these:

1. The universe was created by God who is reasonable, omnipotent, and omniscient.
2. Having once created the world, God left it to work out its destiny; He is therefore a cold, abstract, metaphysical Deity.
3. Human nature is static and uniform.
4. Man now is not different in any important respects from what he was when created.
5. At the creation God made known to man the natural law, which is discoverable by the reason of man.
6. The Christian religion added nothing to this law of nature and is therefore unnecessary.

The defenders of the Church and historical Christianity were not slow to come forward in great numbers; such men as Conybeare, Bentley, Warburton, and Berkeley met the Deists on their own ground and used their own weapons. On the whole the controversy was shallow and lacking in breadth, only Bishop Butler's *Analogy*, which administered the *coup de grâce*, was above the average in intellectual power and moral earnestness.

For once Blake was on the side of the Church, although, in so far as the Church had imbibed any of the Deists' ideas, he attacked her too. We have already seen how forcible he was in denying the omnipotence and even the efficacy of reason, the very basis of the whole Deist structure. Deism was the product of reason and as such was abhorrent to Blake:

> thy religion
> The first author of this war & the distracting of honest minds
> Into confused perturbation & strife & horrour & pride,
> Is a deciet so detestable.[1]

We have also considered his resistance to the current ideas of moral expediency, a conception which showed the Deist influence inside the Church herself. 'He never can be a Friend to the Human Race who is the Preacher of Natural Morality or Natural Religion.'[2] Natural Morality inculcates the 'Selfish Virtues of the Natural Heart. This was the Religion of the Pharisees who murder'd Jesus. Deism is the same & ends in the same',[2] for belief in a self-sufficient human nature, requiring no redemption, leads to self-righteousness and perpetuates 'Tyrant Pride'.[2] From this follows a demand for vengeance for sin, and a religion based upon this conception is the worship of 'Satan under the Name of God',[2] 'their God is Satan, Named by the Divine Name';[2] hence 'Your Religion, O Deists! Deism, is the Worship of the God of this World',[2] which accusation Blake had already levelled at the Church. This insistence on the necessity of punishing sin, instead of forgiving it, is the ultimate cause of war, and so Deism stood further condemned in Blake's eyes because 'All the Destruction, therefore, in Christian Europe has arisen from Deism, which is Natural Religion'.[2] He went on to assert: 'You, O Deists, profess yourselves the Enemies of Christianity, and you are so: you are also the Enemies of the Human Race & of Universal Nature',[3] for they taught that

---

[1] *Vala*, 9. 151–4.   [2] *Jerusalem*, p. 52.
[3] It is rather startling after this to read in the Watson marginalia (p. 6) 'Natural

human nature is static, and that mankind is not different from
when created, thus denying the possibility of change and any
hope of progress. But 'Man is born a Spectre or Satan & is
altogether an Evil, & requires a New Selfhood continually, &
must continually be changed into his direct Contrary',[1] only
then can mankind advance towards the millennium.

Blake's main criticism of Deism is to be found in his pamphlets *There is No Natural Religion*, which he etched in two
series; by means of both, the development of his argument can
be clearly traced.

His first principle was that 'Man's perceptions are not
bounded by organs of perception; he perceives more than sense
(tho' ever so acute) can discover' (11. 1). He thereby implied
that man has a means of knowledge other than the five senses
which are entirely physical; he has in fact the power of spiritual
perception. He continued: 'Man by his reasoning power can
only compare & judge of what he has already perciev'd' (1. 2),
i.e. the function of reason is to systematize experiences already
acquired, and it is limited to the material provided by perception: 'The desires & perceptions of man, untaught by any thing
but organs of sense, must be limited to objects of sense' (1. 6).
But reason supplies nothing that man does not already possess,
for 'from a perception of only 3 senses or 3 elements none could
deduce a fourth or fifth' (1. 3). If there be only natural perception, only natural thoughts can result, and the spiritual is an
illusion. 'None could have other than natural or organic
thoughts if he had none but organic perceptions' (1. 4). But
man's desire is for the life of the spirit—'less than All cannot
satisfy Man' (2. 5)—and he could not have this desire unless he
had some inkling of the object of his desire, for 'none can desire
what he has not perciev'd' (1. 5). The only way to perceive is
by revelation, through poets and prophets (cf. 1. Conclusion),
and above all through the Incarnation, 'therefore God becomes
as we are, that we may be as he is' (2. Application). Blake thus
attempted to refute the basic Deist idea that 'reason is natural
revelation', and to deny any theory that the coming of Christ

Religion is the voice of God', but the following words '& not the result of reasoning
on the Powers of Satan', show that Blake here meant something different from
Deism; he meant that religion itself is natural to man, for 'Man must & will have
Some Religion'. *Jerusalem*, p. 52.

[1] Ibid.

was unnecessary. Trenchant though his argument is, its logic is sometimes doubtful, for it is by no means true that 'none can desire what he has not perciev'd' (1. 5), for a child would still be hungry, if it had not perceived food; although it is tenable that the child would not know that it was food that it desired to satisfy its craving. Nevertheless, this does not substantially affect the argument, which would not suffer if that particular principle were omitted.

From the subject-matter of these pamphlets it is apparent that Blake saw in Deism a close ally of materialism, to which it gave a spurious religious respectability and which he regarded as identical with the rationalist philosophy of Newton. Blake's anti-materialism is nowhere more exquisitely expressed than in his quatrain from the introduction to chapter 3 of *Jerusalem*:

> For a Tear is an Intellectual thing,
> And a Sigh is the Sword of an Angel King,
> And the bitter groan of a Martyr's woe
> Is an Arrow from the Almightie's Bow.

At the same time as he etched these two *Natural Religion* Series, Blake also produced a third tract entitled *All Religions are One*. In this he partly returned to the theme of his previous pamphlets: 'As none by traveling over known lands can find out the unknown, So from already acquired knowledge Man could not acquire more' (4), but his development of it was along a new line. His purpose was to show that 'all Religions . . . have one source' (7). Although this subject is not strictly relevant to the question under discussion, yet, as one critic has declared that this pamphlet 'obviously sweeps away the Revealed Religion, as it was understood by Christian theology',[1] some brief reference to it is required, because if this contention were correct, then it would seem that Blake, whilst knocking the Deists down with one hand, lifted them up again with the other, and agreed with one of their major tenets, thus undermining his previous argument.

All religions and philosophies, according to Blake, have the same origin, from the Universal 'Poetic Genius', or God. He it is who imparts spiritual knowledge to His creatures. But this knowledge is variously appreciated by different nations in

---

[1] J. Middleton Murry, *William Blake*, 1936, p. 20.

different places, 'adapted to the weaknesses of every individual' (3), and according to 'each Nation's different reception of the Poetic Genius' (5). So far from denying revelation, then, Blake would seem to have been affirming it, and all he was asserting was that every religion is but a striving after the One God, and this, of course, is an entirely orthodox conception, Christ being the fulfilment of all.

Although Blake was vitally opposed to Deism, he was always tolerant of its exponents, as he was of any thinker, even when he detested their ideas; so it is not surprising to find that in his marginalia to Watson's *Apology* he defended Paine, a Deist, against the criticism of the bishop. Indeed the notes show that, while rejecting the main Deist position, he accepted the truth of two of their propositions, namely, their views of prophecy and of miracles. His remarks about the former have a very modern ring: 'Prophets, in the modern sense of the word, have never existed. Jonah was no prophet in the modern sense, for his prophecy of Nineveh failed. Every honest man is a Prophet; he utters his opinion both of private & public matters. Thus: If you go on So, the result is So. He never says, such a thing shall happen let you do what you will. A Prophet is a Seer, not an Arbitrary Dictator' (p. 14). With regard to miracles, Blake denied the current definition of 'an arbitrary command of the agent upon the patient' (pp. 12–13). Jesus never performed a miracle in that sense, for 'the Gospel says that Christ could not do a miracle because of Unbelief'. Blake realized that whether our Lord performed miracles or not is quite unimportant, 'for those who believe want not to be confounded by miracles. Christ & his Prophets & Apostles were not Ambitious miracle mongers.' It was Blake's eagerness to discover truth that led him to defend a Deist and accept some of his ideas, but that was as far as he was prepared to go: for the rest of their barren rationalism he had no time.

To the other religious movements of his day Blake was more friendly disposed. Of Irving, who founded the 'Catholic Apostolic Church', Blake remarked to Crabb Robinson, 'He is a highly gifted man—he is a sent man—but they who are sent sometimes go further than they ought.' But it was with the Evangelicals that Blake had most sympathy. Methodism as taught by John Wesley (1703–91) and George Whitefield

(1714–70) was bringing to light many features of the Gospel that the Church was neglecting. Under their influence a great religious revival was taking place, thousands of people being converted at mass meetings to a new devotion to our Lord. In Blake's view one of the primary causes of the deplorable condition of contemporary religion was Puritanism; Voltaire and Rousseau were the leaders in the reaction against it, but they had destroyed not only superstition but even the last vestiges of belief in inspiration and everything beyond abstract virtues. 'No Faith is in all the Earth: the Book of God is trodden under Foot',[1] and men 'mock at Faith and deny Providence'.[2] It was only with the advent of Wesley and Whitefield that

> Faith in God the dear Saviour who took on the likeness of men,
> Becoming obedient to death, even the death of the Cross,[3]

became once again a vital factor in men's lives.

> He sent his two Servants, Whitefield & Westley: were they Prophets,
> Or were they Idiots or Madmen? shew us Miracles!
> Can you have greater Miracles than these? Men who devote
> Their life's whole comfort to intire scorn & injury & death?[4]

Blake made several references to the Evangelical leaders in his works; sometimes to defend them against undeserved attacks, e.g. 'Foote in calling Whitefield, Hypocrite, was himself one; for Whitefield pretended not to be holier than others, but confessed his Sins before all the world';[5]—sometimes to express his approval of them, e.g.

> Whitefield & Hervey guard that Gate, with all the gentle Souls
> Who guide the great Wine-press of Love.[6]

In many respects Blake came near to the Wesleyans; particularly was he akin to them in his rejection of the Church, for he shared their excessive individualism which prevented their achieving an adequate understanding of the nature of the divine society. But always Blake was Blake, his own 'Priest and King' in his

---

[1] *Milton*, 24. 60.
[2] Ibid., 27. 25.
[3] Ibid., 24. 57, 58.
[4] Ibid., 24. 61–25. 2.
[5] *Jerusalem*, 52.
[6] Ibid., 72. 51, 52.

own house; wide though his interests and sympathies may have been, with the Swedenborgians, with the Methodists, with the Irvingites, he remained for the major part of his life aloof from all forms of organized religion. Artistically, and therefore Blake would have said spiritually, this was a great misfortune; 'what his genius required, and what it sadly lacked, was a framework of accepted and traditional ideas which would have prevented him from indulging in a philosophy of his own, and concentrated his attention on the problems of the poet . . . the concentration resulting from a framework of mythology and theology and philosophy is one of the reasons why Dante is a classic, and Blake only a poet of genius'.[1] This judgement has been questioned by another writer on the grounds that 'in the use of tradition Blake exceeded Milton and was second, if to anyone, only to Dante'.[2] It is of course true, one might say obvious, that Blake derived many of his ideas from earlier writers, but his assimilation of them was haphazard; there was no 'framework', nothing but indeterminate selection at the dictate of fancy, whereas 'an authoritative religious tradition tends, particularly in the region of metaphysics, to limit the field of speculation . . . also . . . it disciplines the logical while it restrains the myth-making faculty'.[3]

Conscious rejection of the social and institutional elements in religion tends to an impoverishment in the life of the Churchless individual, showing itself in an incompleteness in humility, a one-sidedness in the truths perceived and expressed, and an excess of individualism unwittingly derived from the very body he repudiates. The free movement of the spirit needs to be balanced by the stability of a tradition in order to prevent its degenerating into eccentricity and dissipating its vitality by an unrestrained diffusiveness. Where this institutional element in a soul's life cannot be traced, we always find either that his religion has always been weak; or that reacting from some religious excess, he is losing his religion; or that he is veering towards some kind of institutionalism; or finally, that his 'religion, though non-institutional, is indeed delicate and deep,

---

[1] T. S. Eliot, *William Blake, Selected Essays, 1917–32*, 1932, p. 308.

[2] M. O. Percival, *William Blake's Circle of Destiny*, 1938, p. 1.

[3] H. C. White, *The Mysticism of William Blake* (University of Wisconsin Studies in Language and Literature, No. 23), 1927, p. 55.

but that this religion was first awakened in this soul by some
fervent institutional religionist'.[1] Blake's religious faith was
never weak, nor was he ever in danger of losing it, nor again
was there any likelihood of his becoming attached to any form
of institutionalism; but undoubtedly he was greatly influenced
by Swedenborg, the founder of a new sect whose social organi-
zation and worship were just as intense as that of any branch of
orthodoxy. It is to Swedenborg we must turn therefore for
further illumination of Blake's religious ideas, though we shall
find cause to regret as the latter's doctrines unfold before us
that Blake was not a more obedient son of the Church and less
of a mental and spiritual syncretist.

[1] Von Hügel, *Eternal Life*, 1912, p. 325.

III
BLAKE AND SWEDENBORG

THE writers with whom Blake has most mental affinity were
Swedenborg, Paracelsus, and Boehme. From them he
gleaned many of his ideas, although he was never a mere
plagiarist; he seized on those theories which he found acceptable, only in order to fuse them in the crucible of his own mind
and represent them with a freshness of interpretation which is
always striking in its originality. Of the three, Swedenborg had
by far the greatest influence on him, and indeed for a short time
Blake was an active member of the New Church, being one of
those who attended the first general conference.

Emanuel Swedenborg, scientist, one time assessor of the
Swedish Board of Mines, theosophist and seer, made the first of
several visits to London in 1710, and in London he died on the
29th of March 1772. At the time of his death his theological
works were not widely known in England, although a translation by John Merchant of chapters 11 to 21 of his *Arcana
Coelestia* had been published by John Lewis at the author's
expense in 1750, and this had been followed in 1763 by an
edition of *The Doctrine of Life for the New Jerusalem*, translated
by W. Cookworthy. Two more works were published in English
during his lifetime: *A Brief Exposition of the Doctrine of the New
Church*, translated by John Merchant, in 1769, and *The Intercourse of the Soul and the Body*, translated by T. Hartley, in 1770.
From then on, interest in him increased; in 1778 *Heaven and Hell*
appeared, also translated by Hartley, and in 1781 *True Christian
Religion*, a two-volume edition, was translated by John Clowes.
The following year a printing society was founded in Manchester
to publish translations of his works in order to propagate his
teaching.

Among the first apostles of Swedenborg in England was
Robert Hindmarsh, who, in the early part of 1782, read several
of his writings, and became so interested in them that he threw
open his house for regular meetings of those who shared his
enthusiasm. The first public meeting was held in the London
Coffee House on Ludgate Hill, on 5 December 1783, and in a

very short time their numbers had increased and included John Flaxman, the sculptor, who became attached to them in the late December of 1783. It is through Flaxman that we have the primary link between Blake and the Swedenborgians, for Stothard introduced Flaxman to Blake in 1780 and the two became the closest of friends.

There would appear to be no certain grounds for the theory that Blake's father was a Swedenborgian and that it was through him that Blake became acquainted with the movement. It was first propounded by Edwin Ellis in 1907, and elaborated eight years later by H. N. Morris, who wrote: 'We know that both (his father and his brother James) were members of the Swedenborgian or New Jerusalem Church in Hatton Gardens, London, and one at least of the "Songs of Innocence" was written by Blake in that Church.' There is no authority for the first part of this sentence at all, beyond the vague reference by Gilchrist to Blake's father as a 'Dissenter', and, moreover, the statement itself is palpably false, although it has been accepted by some critics. Blake's father died in the summer of 1784, three years before the New Church was organized as a separate body, and furthermore, the church in Hatton Gardens was not built until 1797, and was therefore not in existence during his lifetime. It would have been possible for Blake's brother James to have attended the church, but apart from Morris's bare assertion, there is no evidence for it, and Gilchrist's remark that he 'would at times *talk Swedenborg*' implies no more than that he had 'his spiritual and visionary side too.'[1] The second part of Morris's statement is equally false, although according to another writer it is derived from C. A. Tulk, one of the first adherents of the sect and a personal acquaintance of Blake. The poem in question, 'The Divine Image', is one of the *Songs of Innocence*, which were completed in 1789, eight years before the church was erected. Moreover, the church did not become the property of the particular branch of the Swedenborgians with whom Blake was associated until 1800, it being opened for worship on the 16th of February. It does not follow, of course, that Blake's

[1] The sources from which I have pieced together the evidence for refuting Morris's statement include the following: M. R. Lowery, *Yale Studies in English*, xciii. 1940, p. 14; R. Hindmarsh, *The Rise and Progress of the New Jerusalem Church*, 1861, pp. 66, 143; *The Modern Language Review*, xxxviii, 2 April 1943, p. 81; *The New Church Weekly*, London, 1917, xl, p. 413; *The Quest*, 1919, xl, pp. 75, 76.

father was not a Swedenborgian; we do not know; he may
have been a Presbyterian or a Methodist, but a statement based
on such contradictions and only made public some one hundred
and thirty years after the subject's death is of no value whatsoever. What we do know is that Flaxman was a Swedenborgian and through him, and probably through him alone,
Blake was brought into contact with the New Church movement.

At the time when Flaxman joined them the Swedenborgians
had not separated themselves as a religious body from the
Church as a whole; and for worship they usually resorted to the
chapel of the Asylum for Female Orphans in St. George's
Fields, where they were warmly welcomed by the Reverend
Jacob Duché who shared their views. But, being dissatisfied with
their position, they decided to form themselves into a society
distinct from the 'Old Church', and their first meeting as a
separate body took place on 7 May 1787. Their next step was
to acquire a place of worship, and they opened a chapel in
Great East Cheap on 27 January 1788. They followed this by
a project to hold a general conference of all the readers of
Swedenborg's works, and to this end a circular letter was sent
out inviting those who sympathized to attend. There can be
little doubt that Blake received a copy of this, for both he and
his wife were present at the conference, and indeed the presi-
dent, in his opening address, declared: 'It is presumed, that all
present are well acquainted with the design of the present
Meeting, that it is, as stated in the circular letter, for the purpose
of considering the most effectual means of promoting the New
Church.' In any case, Blake knew the contents of the letter,
because it was read out at the conference and was the basis of
the resolutions. As at the time Blake accepted the propositions
listed in the letter, it would be as well to quote several of them
here, without comment for the moment, since they are of value
in illuminating certain of his ideas. It will be seen later how
far Blake absorbed and how far he rejected these various
principles.

> III. That a Trinity of Divine Persons existing from eternity, or
> before the creation of the world, when conceived in idea, is a
> Trinity of Gods, which cannot be expelled by the oral confes-
> sion of one God.

IV. That to believe Redemption to have consisted in the passion of the cross, is a fundamental error of the Old Church.

XIV. That immediately on the Death of the material body, (which will never be re-assumed,) man rises again as to his spiritual or substantial body, wherein he existeth in perfect human form.

XXII. That Miracles are not to be expected at this day, because they carry compulsion with them, and take away man's Free-will in spiritual things.

XXXIV. That external Forms of Worship, agreeable to the doctrines of the New Church are necessary.

XXXV. That the two Sacraments of Baptism and the Holy Supper are essential institutions in the New Church.

XXXVIII. That the Last Judgment was accomplished in the Spiritual World in the year 1757.

The conference began on Easter Monday, 13 April 1789, and continued until the following Friday. Each day the members dined together at a neighbouring tavern in Abchurch Lane, to the number of sixty or seventy, both men and women. Blake, who wrote in an autograph album towards the end of his life that he was 'one who is very much delighted with being in good Company', was no doubt one of the party.

The results of the conference were summed up in a series of resolutions, to which Blake and his wife appended their names, being the thirteenth and fourteenth signatures on the list.

The document begins with a general preamble: 'We whose names are hereunto subscribed do each of us approve of the theological writings of Emanuel Swedenborg, believing that the doctrines contained therein are genuine truths, revealed from heaven, and that the New Jerusalem Church ought to be established distinct and separate from the Old Church.' Then follows the list of resolutions, of which the following are of importance with reference to Blake's theology:

VIII. That it is the opinion of this Conference, that all Faith and Worship directed to any other, than to the one God Jesus Christ in his Divine Humanity, being directed to a God invisible and incomprehensible, have a direct tendency to overturn the Holy Word, and to destroy everything spiritual in the Church.

X. That it is the opinion of this Conference, that the Lord and Saviour Jesus Christ is the only God of Heaven and Earth, and

that his Humanity is Divine . . . that in order to salvation, man
must live a life according to the Ten Commandments.

XXVI. That it is the opinion of this Conference, that the true
Christian Religion is alone to be found in the New Jerusalem
Church, because this is the only Church that acknowledges and
worships Jesus Christ alone, as Father, Son, and Holy Ghost, in
one Divine Person.

In these resolutions and in the propositions taken from the
circular letter, we have briefly outlined several of Swedenborg's
central doctrines, but to appreciate them more fully some
further explication is required, which will also include other of
his beliefs not mentioned in the previously quoted documents.
As far as possible such explication will be given in Swedenborg's own words.

1. *His doctrine of God.* To Swedenborg, with his scientific
background, the idea of God as some vague and indefinite being
was unacceptable. 'It is a vain idea that God is a spirit, if this
means something windy or ethereal.'[1] Accordingly, if we are to
think about God at all, we must use symbols derived from our
own human experience, and so Swedenborg asserted that 'unless
God is thought of and approached as a Man, all idea of Him
perishes; for then the thought is either lost in the contemplation
of empty space, or directed to nature and its objects.'[2] 'All who
think of God from themselves, or from the flesh, think of Him
indeterminately, that is, without any definite idea; but those
who think of God not from themselves, nor from the flesh, but
from the spirit, think of Him determinately; that is, they present
to themselves a conception of the Divine, under the human
form.'[3] Swedenborg developed this idea to the point where he
could declare that 'in all the heavens there exists no other idea
of God than that of man'.[4] God is order, hence man created in
His image and likeness is an image and likeness of order. 'The
whole heaven is a form of divine order on the largest scale, and
is in the sight of God like one man. . . . I have seen as one man
a community of angels consisting of several thousand; this
showed me that heaven in the aggregate is an image of God;
and an image of God is a form of divine order.'[5] 'They who

---

[1] *True Christian Religion*, 621.   [2] Ibid. 538.
[3] *Arcana Coelestia*, 8705.   [4] *Divine Love and Wisdom*, 11.
[5] *True Christian Religion*, 65.

have not a just idea concerning spiritual and heavenly things
are unable to perceive that heavenly and spiritual things are
arranged and conjoined into the form and image of a man.
They think that the earthly and material things, which com-
pose man's outmost nature, make the man, and that without
these man is not man. But let them know that man is not man
from these things, but because he can understand what is true,
and will what is good. These spiritual and heavenly things are
what make man. . . . Man's Intellectual and Voluntary make
the man, and . . . they are in a human form, because they act
in the minutest particulars of the body, as what is internal into
what is external; and therefore, from them man is called an
internal and spiritual man. Heaven itself is such a man, in the
greatest and most perfect form.'[1] This view was not inspired
by a simple anthropomorphism; it means that in the nature of
God there is that 'which alone accounts for the form of heaven
and of man, and the form of every living thing. It is not God
who is thus conceived in the image and likeness of man; it is
man who is conceived in the image and likeness of God.'[2]

The similarity between this teaching and many of Blake's
beliefs is immediately apparent. Blake shared with Swedenborg
the desire to be definite and precise in his conception of spiritual
being.

he who wishes to see a Vision, a perfect Whole,
Must see it in its Minute Particulars, Organized.[3]

Equally with Swedenborg, he rejected all that is vague and
ethereal; 'A Spirit and a Vision are not, as the modern philosophy supposes, a cloudy vapour, or a nothing: they are organized and minutely articulated beyond all that the mortal and
perishing nature can produce.'[4] From this Blake was led on to
the assertion 'Think of a white cloud as being holy, you cannot
love it; but think of a holy man within the cloud, love springs
up in your thoughts, for to think of holiness distinct from man
is impossible to the affections.'[5] The outcome of this train of
thought was for Blake to agree with Swedenborg in his doctrine
of God as Man. 'God is Man & exists in us & we in him.'[6]

---

[1] *Heaven and Hell*, 60.
[2] L. B. de Beaumont, *Spiritual Reconstruction and the Religious Unrest of the Age*,
1918, p. 39.   [3] *Jerusalem*, 91. 20–1.
[4] *Descriptive Catalogue*, iv.   [5] M.D.L.W., p. 12.   [6] *Berkeley*, p. 219.

'Jesus, as also Abraham & David, considered God as a Man in the Spiritual or Imaginative Vision';[1] and in the 'Auguries of Innocence' we find the quatrain:

> God Appears & God is Light
> To those poor Souls who dwell in Night,
> But does a Human Form Display
> To those who Dwell in Realms of day. (129–32.)

Heaven, too, is the form of a man.

> Then those in Great Eternity met in the Council of God
> As one Man, for contracting their Exalted Senses
> They behold Multitude, or Expanding they behold as one,
> As One Man all the Universal family; & that One Man
> They call Jesus the Christ.[2]

In seeking to define the inner life of the Godhead, Swedenborg asserted most emphatically the oneness of God; 'all things of human reason unite and, as it were, concentrate in this, that there is one God, the Creator of the universe.'[3] Nevertheless, there is a Trinity; 'It is plain that there is a divine trinity which consists of Father, Son, and Holy Spirit.'[4] But Swedenborg was so concerned to preserve the idea of unity, which he understood as entirely arithmetical, being characterized by absence of multiplicity,[5] that he objected to the use of the word 'person' with reference to the Trinity, as to his mind it conveyed the idea of personality, and therefore suggested the existence of three Gods, and so he affirmed: 'By three persons I understood three proceeding divine attributes, which are creation, redemption, and generation; that they are the attributes of one God. . . . God is Jesus Christ, who is the Lord Jehovah, from eternity the Creator, in time the Redeemer, and to eternity the Regenerator.'[6] Hence he could declare: 'Before the creation of the world this Trinity did not exist; but after the creation of the world, when God became incarnate, it was provided and came into existence.'[7] So then, Father, Son, and Holy Ghost

---

[1] Ibid., p. 212.   [2] *Vala*, 1. 461–5.

[3] *Divine Love and Wisdom*, 23.   [4] *True Christian Religion*, 164.

[5] Cf. L. Hodgson, *The Doctrine of the Trinity*, 1943, pp. 90–1. Dr. Hodgson points out that any attempt to understand the Trinity in Unity must be based upon an organic conception of unity, not an arithmetical one, the degree of unity being measured 'by a scale of intensity of unifying power' (p. 95).

[6] *True Christian Religion*, 26.   [7] Ibid. 170.

arc but 'three essentials of one God',[1] or 'three Modes of manifestation'.[2]

2. *His doctrines of the Incarnation and Redemption.* It follows from Swedenborg's doctrine of the Trinity that the Incarnation was effected by Jehovah Himself taking flesh in the womb. 'Jehovah God Himself descended and became Man and the Redeemer.'[3] It was rendered necessary because 'faith grounded in love to the Lord',[4] by means of which alone could there be union between man and God, had disappeared from the earth, and 'then the Lord came, and united the Human Essence to the Divine, so that they became entirely one'.[4] As a consequence, there was 'a dispersion of the direful persuasions of falsity, and of the direful lusts of evil'.[4] Redemption consisted in His overcoming temptation, because 'when any one conquers in temptation, he has then inmost communion with God'.[5] So, 'the Lord conquered death, or hell, by combats, which are temptations, and at the same time, by these means, glorified His Human; and the passion of the cross was the last combat or temptation, by which He conquered the one and glorified the other.'[6] Therefore, according to Swedenborg, the passion is distinct from the act of redemption, though the latter is completed by the former. He rejected any idea that 'by the passion of the cross, the Lord took away sins, and made satisfaction to the Father', or that 'He transferred to Himself the sins of those who have faith in Him and that He bore them'.[7] With this repudiation Blake was in full agreement, for, according to Crabb Robinson, he said of the Atonement, 'it is a horrible doctrine. If another man pay your debt, I do not forgive it.'

3. *His doctrine of Providence.* Swedenborg believed that God's guidance or providence was active in the world. 'The operation of the Divine Providence to save man begins at his birth, and continues even to the end of his life, and afterwards to Eternity.'[8] The purpose of divine providence is to reform man, and so bring him to salvation, and it has for its end 'a heaven, consist-

---

[1] *True Christian Religion,* 166.
[2] Blake did not make his attitude to the Trinity very clear; he seems to have been orthodox, but to have used phraseology reminiscent of Swedenborg.
[3] Ibid. 82.   [4] *Arcana Coelestia,* 2034.
[5] *True Christian Religion,* 126.   [6] N.J.L. 12.
[7] Ibid. 15.   [8] *Divine Providence,* 332.

ing of men who have become and are becoming angels'.[1] It works 'silently as an imperceptible stream or a favourable current bears a ship'.[2] This providence does not in any way infringe man's free will, which Swedenborg was at pains to safeguard; indeed, 'it is of the Divine Providence that man should act from freedom according to reason.'[3] Predestination, therefore, is detestable; 'must not that doctrine give rise to cruel ideas concerning God, and to the most shocking opinions concerning religion?'[4] Blake was as much opposed as Swedenborg to any form of predestinarianism, but he considered that, however much he might deny it, Swedenborg did in fact teach it. Hence Blake's remarks in the margin of his copy of *Divine Providence*. 'What could Calvin Say more than is Said in this Number? Final Portion is Predestination' (185). 'Devils & Angels are Predestinated' (203). 'Predestination' (307). Swedenborg, in company with many other able thinkers, of greater mental stature than he, had infinite difficulty in reconciling providence and free will, and while asserting both, he never really achieved a synthesis. It was therefore not difficult for Blake to find inconsistencies in his works. Thus in paragraph 185 of *Divine Providence* Swedenborg wrote: 'they then manifestly see the Divine Providence, and from it their Final Portion, which is that they are to be in hell'; and yet in paragraph 329 he declared, 'all are predestinated or intended for Heaven, and none for Hell.' On the latter, Blake commented, 'Read N. 185 & There See how Swedenborg contradicts himself & N. 69. See also 277 & 203 where he Says that a Place for Each Man is foreseen & at the same time provided.' So it was that Blake, imagining Swedenborg to be upholding predestination, parted company with him on this issue, affirming that 'Predestination after this Life is more Abominable than Calvin's, & Swedenborg is Such a Spiritual Predestinarian . . . Cursed Folly' (277).

4. *His doctrine of Influx.* God is life, and therefore uncreated, for life cannot be created, since to be created is to exist from another, and if life existed from another, there would be another being that would be life. Hence the natural world, and in particular man, exists from the divine and receives its life from

---

[1] Ibid. 27.　　　　[2] Ibid. 186.
[3] Ibid. 97.　　　　[4] *True Christian Religion*, 487.

God. The means by which this life is mediated to man and to
nature is by influx. But life is love and wisdom, 'those two enter
by influx into men's minds, as the heat and light of the sun
enter into their bodies; and they vivify them according to the
recipient forms, each receiving as much as it needs from the
general Influx.'[1]

Blake assimilated little of this teaching, but an occasional
reference indicates that it had some influence on him; thus for
example, he noted on one of Lavater's aphorisms, 'Creation is
God descending according to the weakness of man, for our Lord
is the word of God & every thing on earth is the word of God &
in its essence is God' (630). However, if the doctrine of influx
received little attention from him, he was most eager in his
acceptance of the idea of correspondences, which is closely
related to the conception of influx.[2]

5. *His doctrine of Correspondences.* 'The whole natural order',
wrote Swedenborg, 'corresponds to the spiritual world, not only
the natural world in general, but also in particular. Whatever,
therefore, in the natural world exists from the spiritual, is said
to be its correspondent.'[3] That is to say that there is a positive
relation between the world of causes and the world of effects.
'Man's spiritual world is visible in his natural world.'[4] So close
is this correspondence—'all things which exist in nature, from
the least to the greatest, are correspondents'[5]—that Swedenborg
could detail a list of the parts of a man's body, heart, lungs,
viscera, &c., which correspond with the societies of angels in
the three heavens. But if everything in nature has a spiritual
meaning, the same must apply to words, which in their turn
have an internal or spiritual meaning. So Swedenborg propounded his theory for interpreting Scripture. The Word has
an internal sense 'which in its essence is spiritual, and is within
the external sense, which is natural, as the soul is in the body.
This sense is the spirit which gives life to the letter.'[6] 'Since the
Word interiorly is spiritual and celestial, it is therefore written
by means of pure correspondences',[7] and so a number of his

---

[1] *True Christian Religion*, 364.

[2] Blake accepted the doctrine of Correspondence all the more readily because
it is identical with the 'Astronomia' of Paracelsus and with the 'Signatures' of
Boehme.

[3] *Heaven and Hell*, 89.   [4] Ibid. 91.   [5] Ibid. 106.

[6] N.J.S. 4.   [7] Ibid. 8.

works were commentaries on the books of the Bible, revealing what he believed to be their spiritual meaning.

To Blake this doctrine of correspondence, or 'Divine Analogy'[1] as he sometimes called it, was a method by which he could discover meaning, even amidst the chaos and disunity of the material world. Behind the phenomena of nature he beheld the unchangeable reality of eternity, and declared that

> every Natural Effect has a Spiritual Cause, and Not
> A Natural; for a Natural Cause only seems: it is a Delusion
> Of Ulro & a ratio of the perishing Vegetable Memory.[2]

Thus, in true Swedenborgian manner, he asserted, 'There Exist in the Eternal World the Permanent Realities of Every Thing we see reflected in this Vegetable Glass of Nature.'[3] This conception, Platonic perhaps in origin, but derived directly from Swedenborg, appears repeatedly in the Prophetic books, e.g.

> Even I already feel a World within
> Opening its gates, & in it all the real substances
> Of which these in the outward World are shadows which pass away.[4]

Blake did not use the physical correspondences to any great degree, although he incorporated into his symbolism certain parts of the body, viz. head, heart, and loins, to represent three possible channels of human intercourse with eternity. But following Swedenborg he interpreted the Bible mystically and allegorically; indeed with conscious humour, he said of himself and his opponents

> Both read the Bible day & night,
> But thou read'st black where I read white.[5]

His method of interpretation is seen at its best in the Job series of engravings; in the margin of the first design is displayed prominently the text 'the letter killeth, but the spirit giveth life', and the engravings, so far from illustrating the text literally, tell the story of Job afresh, presenting it as the account of man's spiritual growth, through experience, to union with God.

6. *His doctrine of Degrees.* 'A knowledge of degrees is like a key for uncovering and penetrating into the causes of things.'[6]

---

[1] *Jerusalem*, 85. 7.   [2] *Milton*, 28. 44–6.
[3] *Last Judgment*, pp. 69–70.   [4] *Vala*, 7 a. 363–5.
[5] 'Everlasting Gospel', a. 14.   [6] *Divine Love and Wisdom*, 184.

'Without a knowledge of these degrees nothing can be known of those features which distinguish the three heavens . . . nor without this knowledge of degrees can anything be known of the distinctions which rule in the interior faculties of men's minds . . . and especially of the distinctions between spiritual and natural.'[1]

Degrees are of a twofold order, 'continuous' degrees and 'discrete' degrees. ' "Continuous" degrees is a term applied to the gradual lessening or diminishing from grosser to finer, from denser to rarer.'[2] These represent the more or less of anything, e.g. degrees of temperature ranging from freezing-point to boiling-point. ' "Discrete" degrees are altogether different; they are like things prior, subsequent, and final; or like end, cause and effect.'[2] The end (*causa finalis*) is the purpose for which a thing exists; the cause (*causa efficiens*) is the manner by which it exists; and the effect results from the operation of the cause. No one of these is capable of being changed into either of the other. Thus if we take the series, will, intellect, and action, the will may determine the intellect in a certain direction which issues in a physical activity, yet the will has not become intellectual, nor the intellect an action; they are 'discrete' degrees representing fundamental distinctions.

In God there are three 'discrete' degrees, or degrees of height, 'these are as it were, end the first, end the middle, which is called cause, and end the last which is called effect.'[3] The first is named celestial, the second spiritual, the third natural.

The same three degrees are to be found in man. 'Man, at his birth, first comes into the natural degree, and this increases in him by continuity in accordance with what he learns, and according to understanding acquired by them, to the summit of understanding which is called rational.'[4]

It is here that we find the connexion with Blake, for shortly after it was published he obtained a copy of *Divine Love and Wisdom*, in which the doctrine of degrees is most fully set out, and wrote his annotations in the margins. His most penetrating remarks were with reference to the last passage quoted above. Swedenborg said that the natural degree in man increases 'in accordance with what he learns', which produces understanding,

---

[1] *Divine Love and Wisdom*, 185.　　[2] Ibid. 184.
[3] Ibid. 230.　　　　　　　　　　　　[4] Ibid. 237.

and this develops to the rational. In the copy which Blake possessed the words 'in accordance with what he learns' were translated 'according to the Sciences', and Blake seized on the word 'sciences' to criticize the passage forthwith, declaring that science 'cannot teach intellect'.[1] He then went on to discuss the whole context, saying that it is foolish 'to assert that Man is born in only one degree', and at the same time to maintain that he has three degrees within him. Swedenborg was indeed guilty of an inconsistency here, for later in the same work he declared that man actually has all three degrees in him potentially at birth. In any case Blake considered that two of them 'he must destroy or close up or they will descend', i.e. the end working on the cause produces the effect and descent is made into the natural. But this is not the way in which these degrees operate, for they are discrete and not continuous, and there is therefore no question of descent or ascent. Nevertheless, Blake indicated a weak link in the argument, when he added, 'Is it not also evident that one degree will not open the other . . . but they are discrete & not continuous?' for Swedenborg did use phraseology suggesting that these three degrees are continuous; thus he said: 'It was shown above that there are three degrees of the human mind, termed natural, spiritual, and celestial, and that they can be opened in man one after the other: also, that the first degree to be opened is the natural, and afterwards, if man shuns evils as sins and looks to the Lord, the spiritual degree is opened, and at length the celestial. Since these degrees are opened according to man's life, one after the other, it follows that the two higher degrees may not be opened, and then man remains in the natural, the ultimate, degree.'[2] Blake's criticism was therefore justified. The main interest of this passage lies not in the light it throws upon Blake's theology, for the doctrine of degrees plays no part in his system, but in that it shows clearly that, soon after he had joined the New Church, his mind was already testing Swedenborg's teaching and laying bare its contradictions, thus preparing the way for his eventual rejection of him.[3]

[1] M.D.L.W., pp. 195–6.   [2] *Divine Love and Wisdom*, 248.
[3] This is the only instance where I disagree with Keynes's chronology of Blake's writings, as given in his one-volume edition of 1927. Keynes there assigns the *Divine Love and Wisdom* annotations to 'about 1788'; in so doing he contradicts his previous statement (*The Writings of William Blake*, 1925, 3 vols., vol. i, p. 118) that

7. *His doctrine of Uses.* According to Swedenborg everything exists for a purpose. Love is the end, wisdom is the principal cause, and use is the effect. 'Love and wisdom without the good of use are nothing. . . . Love is nothing without wisdom; for only by means of wisdom does it become really of use; therefore, when love by means of wisdom is expressed in use, it is manifested as something real.'[1] 'It is the same with charity, faith, and works; charity without faith is nothing, and charity and faith without works are nothing; but when expressed in works they become something according to the use of those works.'[2] This is not mere utilitarianism, for use separated from love and wisdom is use no longer. It follows that there must be both good and evil uses, the former from God, the latter from hell. 'Since all good things come from the Lord and all evil things from hell, it follows that none but good uses were created by the Lord and that evil uses arose out of hell.'[2] This doctrine of use applies to the whole of creation. There are uses for sustaining the body, and this includes all things of the vegetable and animal kingdom; there are uses for perfecting the natural, such as science and learning; and there are uses for receiving the spiritual from the Lord, i.e. all the things that have to do with religion.

Blake was attracted by this conception, and devoted one of his minor prophetic books to a lyrical expatiation on this theme. *Thel*, which he wrote in 1789, develops Swedenborg's principle that 'to live for others is to perform uses; uses are the bonds of society and their number is infinite.'[3] Thel, a pre-existent soul, comes down to earth to learn something of the conditions of mortal life; her destiny, she believes, is just to fade away, and have as epitaph the words:

> without a use this shining woman liv'd,
> Or did she only live to be at death the food of worms?[4]

they were written *c.* 1789; nor does he give any reason for the alteration. Yet towards the end of 1789 is almost certainly the correct date, since (i) Blake was still in close contact with the 'society' (vide M.D.L.W., p. 429); (ii) he would hardly have signed his name to an unqualified approval of Swedenborg's writings in April 1789 if previously he had found fault with certain of his tenets as shown in these marginalia.

[1] *True Christian Religion*, 387.
[2] *Divine Love and Wisdom*, 336.
[3] *True Christian Religion*, 746.   [4] *Thel*, ii. 22, 23.

The Cloud answers her:

Then if thou art the food of worms, O virgin of the skies,
How great thy use, how great thy blessing! Every thing that lives
Lives not alone nor for itself.[1]

The Cloud bears food 'to all our tender flowers', and the Clod
of Clay mothers 'the helpless worm', for 'we live not for ourselves'. But as the poem developed, Blake began to doubt the
universal application of this principle. Thel is at last shown the
body she will occupy, and while it may become the food of
worms at death, she can see no use for it during life—there is no
answer to the questions she puts forward, issuing mournfully
from the 'hollow pit'.

Why cannot the Ear be closed to its own destruction?
Or the glist'ning Eye to the poison of a smile?
Why are Eyelids stor'd with arrows ready drawn,
Where a thousand fighting men in ambush lie?
Or an Eye of gifts & graces show'ring fruits & coined gold?
Why a Tongue impress'd with honey from every wind?
Why an Ear, a whirlpool fierce to draw creations in?
Why a Nostril wide inhaling terror, trembling, & affright?
Why a tender curb upon the youthful burning boy?
Why a little curtain of flesh on the bed of our desire?[2]

So the spirit, in fear and trembling, flees back to her eternal
abode.

Once again we see how Blake was probing Swedenborg's
teaching, and although here he did not definitely condemn the
doctrine of uses, he showed that he considered it inadequate to
express the purpose of life, for at the time when *Thel* was written
Blake looked upon the flesh as an impediment to spiritual
progress and therefore of doubtful use.

8. *His doctrine of the Proprium.* It is one of the central teachings
of the Christian faith that self-love is the root of all sin; Swedenborg reproduced this doctrine in his idea of the proprium. The
proprium is the selfhood. 'This proprium is the love of self and
thence the love of the world, or the love of the world and thence
the love of self.'[3] 'Self-love is to will well to self alone, and not
others, except for the sake of self, not even to the Church, one's

---

[1] Ibid. 25–7.   [2] Ibid. iv. 11–20.
[3] *Divine Providence*, 206.

country, or any human society.'[1] 'The selfhood of man is nothing but evil; wherefore he who attaches what is Divine to himself as his own, not only defiles but profanes it.'[2] Self-love is indeed original sin. 'In proportion as any one is in the love of self, in the same proportion he is being led by himself . . . he is being led by his proprium, and a man's proprium is only evil; it is, indeed, his hereditary evil, and this is to love self more than God, and the world than heaven.'[3] This self-love issues in the hatred of one's neighbour, in envy, contempt for others, and enmity against those who do not show one favours, and ultimately it produces a desire for 'a career of universal dominion, not only over the world but also over heaven, and indeed over God himself'.[4]

Blake accepted the truth of this without reserve; a large number of his poems are variations on the theme of

A World in which Man is by his Nature the Enemy of Man,
In pride of Selfhood.[5]

'In Selfhood', he believed, 'we are nothing, but fade away in morning's breath.'[6] Even love itself is self-seeking, unless a death to self has been achieved. It is the excising of the selfhood which is the main feature of the whole process of regeneration; hence Blake wrote 'Regeneration' by the side of Lavater's aphorism: 'The energy of choice, the unison of various powers for one is only WILL, born under the agonies of self-denial and renounced desires' (20). He prayed to Jesus:

O Saviour pour upon me thy Spirit of meekness & love!
Annihilate the Selfhood in me: be thou all my life![7]

The whole of existence is an example and warning of the errors of the selfhood: 'The Man is himself become a piteous example of oblivion.'[8] To appreciate this is to take the first step towards the destruction of the false self in order that the universal self might be realized.

9. *States.* In Swedenborg's theology the doctrines of states did not receive much emphasis, but, as it had a prominent position in Blake's system, some reference to it is required, since

---

[1] *Heaven and Hell*, 556. [2] *Apocalypse Revealed*, 758.
[3] N.J.H.D. 70. [4] *True Christian Religion*, 400.
[5] *Jerusalem*, 43. 52, 53. [6] Ibid. 45. 13.
[7] Ibid. 5. 21, 22. [8] Ibid. 45. 8, 9.

it seems likely that he derived the germ of his conception from Swedenborg. Every man may progress through three states. 'Man's first state, which is a state of damnation, every one has hereditarily from his parents; for man is born therefrom into the love of self and the love of the world, and from these as fountains into evils of every kind.'[1] Men are in it 'who do not suffer themselves to be regenerated'. The second state is one of reformation, 'in which he begins to think of heaven on account of the joy there'; he enters the second state 'when he begins to think there is such a thing as sin'. The third state, that of regeneration, 'takes up and continues the former state. It begins when man desists from evils as sins, and progresses as he shuns them, and it is perfected as he fights against them; and then, so far as he conquers from the Lord, he is regenerated.'[1] There are, in addition, various states in which no man can be reformed; they are 'states of fear, of misfortune, of disordered mind, of bodily disease, of ignorance, and of blindness of the understanding', i.e. they are 'states of non-liberty and non-rationality'.[2] The term 'state' is further applied to man's natural or external condition, and to his spiritual and internal condition. Blake believed that this idea had Biblical authority, and incorporated it into his ethics, in order to avoid moral condemnation, the error lying with the state, and not so much with the individual:

> Iniquity must be imputed only
> To the State they are enter'd into.[3]

This, he held, was the only way to condemn the sin and yet forgive the sinner. Man passes through these states like a traveller, and need not remain in any unless he so wills. Blake had thus taken Swedenborg's teaching and developed it along very different lines. What to Swedenborg was a condition from which a man may be delivered by a knowledge of sin, to Blake was a condition which excuses the sinner for his misdoings; and what to Blake was a passing phase of little importance, to Swedenborg was a situation which is frequently unchangeable.

10. *Ethics.* Finally there remain two aspects of Swedenborg's

---

[1] *Divine Providence*, 83.   [2] Ibid. 138.
[3] *Jerusalem*, 49. 65, 66.

ethics to be passed under review, viz. his acceptance of the
decalogue as the norm of conduct, and his teaching on sex.

We have already seen how the members of the New Church
believed that 'in order to salvation, man must live a life according to the Ten Commandments', and this belief was strongly
supported by their master. 'The commandments of the
Decalogue', according to him, 'are an epitome of the whole of
religion, by which communion of God with man, and of man
with God, is effected. Hence their supreme holiness.'[1] It was
Blake's conviction that Jesus had freed mankind from subservience to the law, or decalogue, and had trodden underfoot the
'poisoned rock',[2] breaking all ten commandments; indeed 'no
virtue can exist without breaking these ten commandments'.[3]
So Blake had little sympathy with Swedenborg's judgement,
and indeed soon began to suspect that he was equally infected
with the moralism that Blake so deplored in the contemporary
Church; to that extent, he was 'the Samson shorn by the
Churches',[4] which had 'perverted Swedenborg's Visions',[5]
because they had imbued him with their own pestilential
legalism, and so his works showed

> the Transgressors in Hell, the proud Warriors in Heaven,
> Heaven as a punisher, & Hell as One under Punishment,
> With Laws from Plato & his Greeks to renew the Trojan Gods,
> In Albion, & to deny the value of the Saviour's blood.[6]

To Crabb Robinson Blake said of Swedenborg, 'parts of his
scheme are dangerous. His sexual religion is dangerous.' But
Swedenborg's attitude to sex was a highly exalted one. In
contrast to the grossly animal conception of sex accepted by
eighteenth-century society, he taught with open sincerity the
purity of the sex act within the sanctity of the marriage bond.
Sex is a means of union or conjunction. 'For the male and
female were so created that from two they may become as one
man, or one flesh; and when they become one, then taken
together they are man in his fullness; but without this conjunction they are two, and each is as it were a divided or half-man.'[7]
He distinguished between the love of sex which pertains to the

[1] *True Christian Religion*, 283.   [2] *Ahania*, 11 d. 5.
[3] *Marriage of Heaven and Hell*, p. 23.
[4] *Milton*, 24. 50.   [5] Ibid. 46.
[6] Ibid. 51–4.   [7] *Conjugal Love*, 37.

natural man, and conjugal love which pertains to the spiritual man. The one is entirely physical and external, the other is of God and internal, so much so that the latter 'remains after death with those that come into heaven'.[1] Nevertheless, con-jugal love has its physical aspect, for 'a married pair who mutually and reciprocally love each other inwardly, in mind, also mutually and reciprocally love each other as to their bodies'.[2] With all this Blake was fundamentally in agreement. As man, he believed, was originally androgynous, and the division into sexes was a result of the Fall, he shared Sweden-borg's idea that the sexual union of man and woman is an approach to the ideal, and that neither is complete without the other. It is true that Blake occasionally made statements which seem to advocate 'free love', but he did not employ the term in its modern sense as mere carnal connexion, which can degrade love into lust, rather with the meaning that in the ideal society marriage will be unnecessary; it is probably on this account that Blake found fault with Swedenborg, because the latter con-ceived of the nuptial state continuing in heaven, whereas the former affirmed that 'In Eternity they neither marry nor are given in marriage'.[3]

This brief review of Swedenborg's chief doctrines should now enable us to examine the nature of Blake's relation to him and to assess the contribution which he made to the poet's thought.

Blake, as we have already noted, became a member of the New Church in 1789, and attended its first general conference. He was also present at one or more meetings of the society, at which Swedenborg's works were discussed.[4] At the same time he was occupied in reading the writings for himself. We know that he read *True Christian Religion, Divine Love and Wisdom, Divine Providence*, and possibly the *Worship and Love of God*, and it is almost certain that he read *Heaven and Hell*.[5] But by means of this study he began to discover that Swedenborg was not the

[1] Ibid. 38.　　　　　　　　　　　[2] *Apocalypse Revealed*, 983.
[3] *Jerusalem*, 34. 15.　　　　　　　[4] M.D.L.W., p. 429.
[5] One painting listed in *Descriptive Catalogue* was taken from *True Christian Religion*. *Divine Love and Wisdom* and *Divine Providence* are both annotated. *The Worship and Love of God* is said to have been on a 'list of books to be read' written on a sketch (*Morning Light*, xxvi, 1903, p. 119). H. N. Morris (*The Quest*, xi, 1919, p. 80) asserts that he read *Apocalypse Revealed*, and, as proof, says he annotated it; there is no record of this.

divine teacher he at first thought him to be. In 1788, in his copy of Lavater, he underlined the aphorism 'Who adheres to a sect has something of its cant' (339), and this was perhaps the unconscious beginning of his progressive repudiation of Swedenborg. The notes which he wrote in the margin of his copy of *Divine Love and Wisdom*, in 1789, are quite restrained. 'Surely this is an oversight' (p. 24), he commented on one passage; but in 1790, when he annotated *Divine Providence*, his tone had become more trenchant. 'Lies & Priestcraft' (pp. xviii–xix), he declared, and again, 'Cursed Folly' (277). In these two years his thought underwent a marked change, which was probably not unconnected with the influence of the revolutionary coterie with whom he associated at bookseller Johnson's. Among the free-thinkers who came to weekly dinners at No. 72 St. Paul's Churchyard was Dr. Priestley, who attacked Swedenborg in his *Letters to the Members of the New Church*, published in 1791. Before their publication, Priestley had sought information from Hindmarsh, who sent such copies of Swedenborg's works as he was requested to Johnson's shop.[1] There were no doubt heated discussions about Swedenborg, in which Drs. Price and Priestley, Fuseli, Godwin, and Blake himself joined.

However, apart from this anti-Swedenborgian influence, which must not be overrated in a man so independent in thought as Blake, he found himself diverging from Swedenborg in many respects, a divergence which he expressed in his *Marriage of Heaven and Hell*, which was probably written in 1790, although not etched until 1793. Blake had indeed derived the idea of this work from Swedenborg himself, for he had noted on page 56 of *Divine Love and Wisdom*, 'Good & Evil are here both Good & the two contraries Married'; and on page 458, 'Heaven & Hell are born together.' Swedenborg's thesis was that God acts, man reacts. Man perceiving this reaction believes it to be his own doing, not realizing it is of God, and, being self-centred, he reacts against God. But if he believes that all this life is from God, and all the good in life comes from the action of God, and that all the evil derives from the reaction of man against God, then he can give up reacting from himself and react from God's action. Blake misunderstood this, because he

---

[1] Hindmarsh, op. cit., p. 132.

equated reaction with evil, and did not see that reaction itself is neutral, and that it is good or evil according to whether it is from man's hereditary evil or from the action of God.[1] However, although based on a misinterpretation, the *Marriage of Heaven and Hell* took its inception from these notes.

The Marriage of Heaven and Hell is a satire on Swedenborg, written in the latter's style and with the latter's typical arrangement; thus after a few pages of argument there follows a Memorable Fancy, which purports to be a vision and sums up the previous thesis. The book is prefaced by an Argument, and then opens with the words: 'As a new heaven is begun, and it is now thirty-three years since its advent, the Eternal Hell revives' (p. 3). This is a reference to the New Heaven, whose advent in 1757 Swedenborg had proclaimed, but Blake caustically suggested that the spirit of revolt which had been apparent since that date must indicate the revival of the 'Eternal Hell' and not the 'New Heaven'. His criticism of Swedenborg was then developed on various grounds. He is first charged with moralism and with the mistake of trying to eliminate evil in the interest of good; secondly, with over-emphasis on reason; thirdly, with spiritual pride, and lastly with lack of originality. Under these four heads we have Blake's main reasons for rejecting him.

'The highest harmony', according to Aristotle, 'springs from opposites, and all things are in a state of strife.' This was Blake's own considered opinion. 'Without Contraries is no progression. Attraction and Repulsion, Reason and Energy, Love and Hate, are necessary to Human existence' (p. 3). It is the height of error to try 'to make One Family of Contraries'.[2] Hence Blake scorned the attempt to drive out all that is evil on the grounds that 'a man cannot do good which is truly so until evil is put away'.[3] Moreover, Blake saw in this line of thought the domination of reason, and 'Swedenborg was wrong in endeavouring to explain to the *rational* faculty what the reason cannot comprehend' was Blake's remark to Crabb Robinson, 'he should have left that'. Swedenborg tried to demonstrate the

---

[1] This theory of action and reaction was used by Blake in one passage, viz. *Jerusalem*, 29. 9–18, where Satan is called the Reactor and is said to have 'founded his Reaction into a Law of Action'.

[2] *Jerusalem*, 55. 15.   [3] *True Christian Religion*, 435.

reasonableness of his doctrines, although presenting them as revealed truths, but the perception of spiritual reality is outside the scope of reason, according to Blake, and so he condemned Swedenborg as but another child of the Age of Reason.

Insistence on reason tends to produce pride, of which Blake further accused Swedenborg. His ideas are 'conceited notions' (p. 22). 'Swedenborg boasts that what he writes is new. . . . A man carried a monkey about for a show, & because he was a little wiser than the monkey, grew vain, and conciev'd himself as much wiser than seven men. It is so with Swedenborg: he shows the folly of churches, & exposes hypocrites, till he imagines that all are religious, & himself the single one on earth that ever broke a net' (p. 21). But so far from this being so, he has merely reproduced the ideas of others: 'Swedenborg has not written one new truth . . . he has written all the old falshoods . . . thus Swedenborg's writings are a recapitulation of all superficial opinions and an analysis of the more sublime, but no further' (p. 22). Blake had been led to this conclusion by his current reading of the works of Boehme and Paracelsus. 'Any man of mechanical talents may, from the writings of Paracelsus or Jacob Behmen, produce ten thousand volumes of equal value with Swedenborg's . . . but when he has done this, let him not say that he knows better than his master, for he only holds a candle in the sunshine' (ibid.).

We find then that Blake repudiated Swedenborg because of his attitude to reason and to nature;[1] because of his supposed predestinarianism; because of his approval of the law; because of his pride and so-called plagiarism. A further contributory cause was the attitude of his followers to corporate worship and the Sacraments, which they upheld but which Blake rejected. Nevertheless, Blake had derived much from him, and some nineteen years later he could recommend his works to artists as a source of imaginative stimulus. 'The works of this visionary are well worthy the attention of Painters and Poets; they are foundations for grand things.'[2] Towards the end of his life, he said to Crabb Robinson: 'He was a divine teacher—he has

[1] One of his notes on the Illustrations to Dante (Design 7) reads: 'Swedenborg does the same [i.e. makes "The World the Foundation of All"] in saying that in this World is the Ultimate of Heaven. This is the most damnable Falshood of Satan & his Antichrist.'
[2] *Descriptive Catalogue*, viii.

done much good, and will do much good—he has corrected many errors of Popery, and also of Luther and Calvin.' So, as the years passed, Blake saw Swedenborg more in perspective, as a man to whom he was much indebted and from whom he had derived many ideas which bore fruit in his own works, but with whom he could never be in entire agreement.

According to one report 'Blake informed Tulk that he had two different states; one in which he liked Swedenborg's writings, and one in which he disliked them. The first was a state of pride in himself, and then they were distasteful to him, but afterwards he knew that he had not been wise and sane. The second was a state of humility, in which he received and accepted Swedenborg.'[1] Tulk was a friend of Blake, but we have already seen reason to doubt one report said to emanate from him, and here again we must demur before accepting this statement at its face value. In the first place, it is at third hand; in the second place, the categories of pride and humility, in the sense used here, were by no means acceptable to Blake; and in the third place, the words read more like a Swedenborgian apologia than the original utterance of the poet.

Blake himself, perhaps, best summed up his relationship with Swedenborg, when he wrote in *The Marriage of Heaven and Hell*, 'OPPOSITION is true Friendship' (p. 20).

[1] *New Church Magazine*, May 1887.

IV

BLAKE AND MYSTICISM

IF anyone, unacquainted with the works of the great mystics, were to be presented with a copy, for example, of the *Divine Names* or the *Mystical Theology* of the Pseudo-Dionysius, he would no doubt be at a loss to appreciate them or even to understand them, for the mystics have a language and a method of expression peculiar to themselves. Their approach to reality, though it can still be interpreted theologically, is at once more devotional and more intense than that of the dogmatic theologian. It is more devotional because it springs directly from personal experience, and owes little or nothing to theory. It is more intense for the self-same reason; having had contact with the absolute, they strain their vocabulary to the utmost in an endeavour to convey some glimpse of what they have so vividly apprehended. Hence their great emphasis—and sometimes from the dogmatist's point of view their over-emphasis—on those aspects of the truth which they have absorbed the most and which they can, therefore, the most easily express. Hence also the use made not infrequently of symbolism; the divine vision is such that the words of everyday speech, with their plethora of mundane associations, are inadequate to present the full truth, and so a resort is made to symbolism, in an attempt to escape the constriction and inexactitude of ordinary language.

Mystical writers are of two kinds. On the one hand, there is the type, exemplified by St. Teresa, that is chiefly concerned with the interior experiences of the soul, and the psychological factors regulating the states of contemplation. On the other hand, there is the type, of which St. Augustine is the supreme example, that is not satisfied with this subjectivism and manifests a metaphysical passion issuing in an earnest attempt to give an exact description coupled with a philosophical and theological interpretation of the reality perceived. In the great mystics these two elements are conjoined, and there is a constant interplay between an adoring communion with God and an objective reading of the experience.

These considerations have severally to be borne in mind when seeking to interpret the theology of any mystic. The same applies to William Blake, if he be a mystic, and therefore, before we can finally set out to formulate his doctrines, it is necessary to find the answers to three questions. What is mysticism? to what extent was Blake a mystic? and what effect, if any, had his mysticism on his theological ideas and the forms under which he expressed them?

In attempting to define mysticism we must beware of being influenced by preconceived ideas. That is to say, that if we have any reason to think Blake a mystic, we must not give a meaning to the word 'mysticism' that will automatically entitle him to be classified as such. To avoid this, and rather than reproduce one or more of the many definitions which have been given of mysticism, it would be as well to turn to the mystics themselves and consider their own testimony as to their purpose and aim. 'The end I have in view is the divine Embracing, the union of the soul with the Divine Substance. In this loving, obscure knowledge God unites Himself with the soul eminently and divinely.' 'This knowledge consists in a certain contact of the soul with the Divinity, and it is God Himself Who is then felt and tasted, though not manifestly and distinctly, as it will be in glory.' Thus far St. John of the Cross, and from Pseudo-Dionysius: 'Do thou, in the intent practice of mystic contemplation, leave behind the senses and the operations of the intellect, and all things that the senses or the intellect can perceive, and all things which are not and all things which are, and strain upwards in unknowing, as far as may be, towards the union with Him Who is above all being and knowledge.' 'The sweetness of contemplation', says St. Gregory, 'is worthy of love exceedingly, for it carries away the soul above itself, it opens out things heavenly, and shows that things earthly are to be despised; it reveals things spiritual to the eyes of the mind, and hides things bodily.' 'Nought more profitable,' declares Richard Rolle, 'nought merrier than grace of contemplation, the which lifteth us from low things and presenteth us to God.' We conclude from these passages that mysticism, or contemplation, is an experience and perception of the Being and Presence of God, and that above all it is union with God.

In the West, contemplation has always been linked with

asceticism. 'No one can be enlightened unless he be first cleansed or purified and stripped', said the author of the *Theologia Germanica* in words which exactly express the thought of all the great Catholic mystics. But this conjunction cannot be regarded as always essential. There have been ascetics who were not mystics, and there have been mystics who were not ascetics. Especially is this to be noted of those who were mystics and at the same time artists. These men, of whom Blake is a leading example, have always to face the problem of creativity. 'Creativeness requires that a man should forget about his own moral progress and sacrifice his personality. . . . If a man feels nothing but humility and a perpetual sense of sin, he can do no creative work.'[1] 'Unity & Morality', said Blake, 'are secondary considerations, & belong to Philosophy & not to Poetry.'[2] It is paradoxical that asceticism absorbs a man in himself, making him concentrate on his own moral improvement, whereas creativeness makes him forget himself. Hence, 'the greatness of creative genius is not correlative to moral perfection. . . . Creative genius is not concerned with salvation or perdition.'[3] But if the only true path is that of holiness, what of the man who devotes himself to art? The crux of the problem lies in the answer we give to the question whether humility is the only true foundation of the spiritual life, or whether there is another on which creative energy may base itself. The poet or artist does not start from humility, inveighing against the burden of sin and the weakness of his nature; his spiritual condition is rather that of a superabundance of creative energy. At the moment of creation man feels a victory over sin; humility and asceticism have no further place, inspiration predominates. But, 'Creation may acquire a religious meaning and justification, if, in the phenomenon of inspiration, man is responding to a divine call to co-operate with divine creation.'[4] Thus the way of asceticism and that of creativeness are seen to lead ultimately to the same goal; both achieve a liberation from the selfhood, the one by purgation, the other by entire self-transcendence and self-forgetfulness in the act of creation, and

[1] N. Berdyaev, *The Destiny of Man*, 1937, p. 168.
[2] *On Homer's Poetry.*
[3] N. Berdyaev, *The Destiny of Man*, 1937, p. 167.
[4] Id., *Freedom and the Spirit*, 1935, p. 231.

so 'the path of creativeness is also a path to moral and religious perfection, a way of realizing the fullness of life'.[1]

It was this problem that Blake, as a mystic and an artist, had to face. At the outset of his career, believing that asceticism and contemplation are indivisibly connected, he determined to regiment himself and force his character into the true ascetic mould. His notes on Lavater reveal a moral sensitivity which even the desert fathers would have commended. 'Uneasy; this I know not' (514). 'Very Uneasy indeed, but *truth*' (518). 'Uneasy: this I lament that I have done' (486). 'Uneasy, but I hope to mend' (588). 'Uneasy, yet I hope I should not do it' (449). To stimulate himself to repentance and to further moral effort, he repeatedly recalled to mind his 'past sins, for these a man should never avert his thoughts from' (523). Such behaviour was entirely opposed to Blake's genius; he soon learned from experience that asceticism was not the way for him. Nevertheless, he was loath to condemn it outright, and in *The Marriage of Heaven and Hell*, which he wrote while still confused with indecision, he tried to find a place for it, on the pretext that mortification, while of no value to the individual who practises it, may yet be a means of leading others into the way of truth. Thus Ezekiel ate dung and 'lay so long on his right & left side' because of his desire to raise 'other men into a perception of the infinite'. 'Is he honest', asks the prophet, 'who resists his genius or conscience only for the sake of present ease or gratification?' (p. 13). Here indeed was the rub, as far as Blake was concerned; he could not resist his genius and so he finally rejected asceticism. Unfortunately, having put it aside as unsuitable to himself, he was unable to see that it may well be adapted to others unendowed with creative genius, and therefore he condemned it completely, believing that Mohammedanism had been providentially ordained to counteract the withering effect of ascetic Christianity. To his mind the condemnation of asceticism involved the condemnation of Christianity as a whole. His situation was intolerable; believing the Gospel to be true, he was yet compelled to reject it. No wonder he declared that

Men understand not the distress & the labour & sorrow
That in the Interior Worlds is carried on in fear & trembling,[2]

[1] Id., *Destiny of Man*, 1937, p. 169.   [2] *Jerusalem*, 59. 50, 51.

for who, among his friends and contemporaries, could have understood his difficulties, quite apart from being able to give him any aid?

It was with mental travail and after arduous spiritual struggle that Blake eventually arrived at his solution. 'I have indeed fought thro' a Hell of terrors and horrors (which none could know but myself) in a divided existence; now no longer divided nor at war with myself, I shall travel on in the strength of the Lord God, as Poor Pilgrim says.'[1] Blake's final solution was twofold. In the first place, he persisted in his rejection of asceticism. The medieval mystics, e.g. St. John of the Cross, St. Rose of Lima, and St. Bernard, are almost repellent with their incredible austerities, with their inhuman treatment of their bodies. Their conduct suggests Manichaean dualism rather than orthodox Christianity, and their rejection of all human ties seems to make nonsense of the Incarnation. Nevertheless, these same mystics were true to the logic of their faith in a crucified God. To follow Jesus means to follow the way of the Cross; to be one with Christ involves sharing His pain and having fellowship with His suffering. They lost their life to save it; as members of Christ's Body, they shared in His atonement, offering themselves in union with the Crucified. So that while we may condemn their excesses as rooted in a dualist conception, we cannot but admire their strong personal love for Jesus and their eagerness to give all, expecting nothing in return, their ardent desire to present themselves to God for His sake alone. 'O Love,' declared St. Catherine of Genoa, 'I do not wish to follow Thee for the sake of these delights, but solely from a motive of true love.' While Blake doubtless admired their fervour, he set himself adamantly against the length to which they carried their practice of it. 'No one bruises or starves himself to make himself fit for labour.'[2] Towards the end of his life he summed up his experience in writing to his friend Linnell: 'No discipline will turn one Man into another, even in the least particle, & such discipline I call Presumption & Folly. I have tried it too much not to know this, & am very sorry for all such who may be led to such ostentatious Exertion against their Eternal Existence itself, because it is Mental Rebellion against the Holy Spirit, & fit only for a Soldier of

---

[1] *To Hayley*, 4 Dec. 1804.   [2] *Jerusalem*, 17. 21.

Satan to perform.'[1] Having thus rejected all asceticism, Blake disassociated it from Christianity, regarding it as an alien strand in the Gospel, and affirmed that 'Christianity is Art',[2] i.e. that the way of creativeness is the way of salvation. By this means he was enabled to find a basis for creativity in Christianity. His solution was, however, only partial, for asceticism has a place in Christian life; Blake's failure to appreciate this was largely occasioned by his isolation from the Church, communion with which would have counterbalanced the exaggerated emphases to which he was led by his sturdy independence.

In view of these considerations, it is unlikely that we shall find that Blake's mysticism followed the traditional pattern of the Catholic mystics.

The various symbolic forms adopted by the mystics to describe their efforts to attain to union with God have this in common, that they all outline certain distinct stages in their quest; this is true whether their imagery be that of a pilgrimage as in Dante or Bunyan, or whether it be that of a marriage as in St. Bernard or Richard of St. Victor. The number of stages differs from mystic to mystic, each has his or her individual plan; thus Blessed John Ruysbroeck has seven, Hugh of St. Victor four, and Walter Hilton, following the time-honoured division of the Mystic Way, has three; while Evelyn Underhill considers mysticism under five heads. With the exercise of much ingenuity, this last classification has been applied to Blake, even to the extent of detailing which poems belong to which stage; but this is to look for precision where none can be found. Although there are certain clearly recognizable steps in the growth of the mystic consciousness, it is untrue to life to separate them sharply from one another, for they are seldom unmixed in form and not infrequently they merge together, periods of illumination, for example, being intermitted with those of purgation. Furthermore, Blake had his own individual scheme, in which there were three stages, and as was natural for a man whose mysticism was so closely connected with his art and whose system was founded upon a creative response to the divine call and not upon an ascetic one, he symbolized the quest as a gradual cleansing of vision, the separate phases of

[1] 1 Feb. 1826. [2] Laocoon.

which are twofold, threefold, and fourfold vision—single vision being the condition of those who have not yet entered upon the mystic way. However, Blake, whose mysticism was practical, not theoretic, was far from precise in outlining his ascent to reality; the exact significance to be attached to the various kinds of vision is not always evident; accordingly, in what follows, though an attempt is made to give a more or less systematic outline of Blake's conception of the mystic way, it must not be forgotten that such an exposition is at best diagrammatic and only answers loosely to the experience underlying Blake's poetic and pictorial work.

Single vision is the condition of the man who is concerned only with that which is outward, with the material, and whose philosophy is merely a rationalization of the perceptions received through the five senses. As such he is unable to apprehend or enjoy any communion with the world of eternity, which is 'incomprehensible To the Vegetated Mortal Eye's perverted & single vision'.[1]

The Visions of Eternity, by reason of narrowed perceptions,
Are become weak visions of Time & Space, fix'd into furrows of
    death.[2]

The human mind unites the self not with things as they really are but with images and aspects of things. 'The verb "to be" which he uses so lightly, does not truly apply to any of the objects amongst which the practical man supposes himself to dwell.'[3] Man takes his own sensations for qualities inherent in the objects of the external world and, selecting some and discarding others according to the dictates of his temperament, preconceptions, environment, and mental limitations, he constructs his own universe. He then forgets that this pattern he has made is merely a representation and not reality itself, that this sense world is not the real external universe but the self's projected picture of it, and that the slightest alteration in the rhythm of the senses would present a totally new range of matter. 'By false desires and false thoughts man has built up for himself a false universe: as a mollusc, by the deliberate and persistent absorption of lime and rejection of all else, can build

---

[1] *Jerusalem*, 53. 10, 11.   [2] Ibid. 49. 21, 22.
[3] E. Underhill, *Practical Mysticism*, 1931, p. 5.

up for itself a hard shell which shuts it from the external world, and only represents in a distorted and unrecognisable form the ocean from which it was obtained. This hard and wholly unnutritious shell, this one-sided secretion of the surface-consciousness, makes as it were a little cave of illusion for each separate soul.'[1] So it was Blake's fervent prayer:

> May God us keep
> From Single vision & Newton's sleep.[2]

To the man of single vision, the world of his own creating becomes a barrier to his contact with reality. It is this fact which explains in part Blake's attitude to nature. 'Nature', he told Crabb Robinson, 'is the work of the Devil', for 'everything is *Atheism* which assumes the reality of the natural and un-spiritual world', nature being nothing more than an 'excre-mentitious Husk & Covering'[3], 'an outside shadowy Surface superadded to the real Surface'.[4] So he maintained that 'Natural Objects always did & now do weaken, deaden & obliterate Imagination in Me';[5] and to Fuseli he remarked 'Nature puts me out'. Hence it is not surprising that he de-clared 'The Natural Earth & Atmosphere is a Phantasy'.[6] Once man has been awakened to his plight, the way of escape lies open, viz. through detachment and self-annihilation. Both of these are categories of asceticism, but they were achieved by Blake, not through purgation, but by the affirmation of his genius under the direction, as he would have said, of the Holy Spirit.

Blake's detachment from the material things of life is amusingly illustrated by the difficulty his wife found in broach-ing the subject of domestic finance, her method of drawing attention to their depleted resources being to place an empty platter in front of her money-hating husband. 'Were I to love money,' he said, 'I should lose all power of thought! desire of gain deadens the genius of man.' So he admonished his readers:

> Crave not for the mortal & perishing delights, but leave them
> To the weak, and pity the weak as your infant care.[7]

---

[1] Id., *Mysticism*, 14th ed., 1942, pp. 198, 199.
[2] *To Butts*, 22 Nov. 1802.
[3] *Jerusalem*, 98. 18, 19.
[4] Ibid. 83. 47.
[5] Wordsworth, p. 44.
[6] M.D.L.W., p. 285.
[7] *Milton*, 27. 56, 57.

'He took no thought for life, what he should eat,' reads his obituary notice in the *Literary Gazette*, 'or what he should drink; nor yet for his body, what he should put on; but had a fearless confidence in the Providence which had given him the vast range of the world for his recreation and delight.'

Although Blake repudiated the ascetic practices of the great mystics, he was entirely in agreement with Father Augustine Baker in affirming that the selfhood must be destroyed before there can 'enter into the soul the Divine love and Divine will, and take possession thereof'. The man who would ascend to God must do so 'by Self annihilation back returning to Life Eternal',[1] for the selfhood is the enemy of the divine. 'Thy Selfhood is for ever accursed from the Divine presence.'[2] The 'Great Selfhood' is Satan himself, of whose nature all created beings partake in so far as they have not beaten 'these hypocritic Selfhoods on the Anvils of bitter Death'.[3] To Blake the individuality was immortal and distinct from the selfhood which is the individuality's outer coating of error, and which

is a false Body, in Incrustation over my Immortal
Spirit, a Selfhood which must be put off & annihilated alway,[4]

and which affects the whole of the unregenerate man's life, to such an extent that even a visit to the theatre can feed his pride. 'At a trajic scene The soul drinks murder & revenge & applauds its own holiness.'[5] The destruction of this incrustation is the great theme of *Milton*:

I will go down to self annihilation and eternal death,
Lest the Last Judgment come & find me unannihilate
And I be seiz'd & giv'n into the hands of my own Selfhood. (15. 22-4.)

I come to Self Annihilation.
Such are the Laws of Eternity, that each shall mutually
Annihilate himself for others' good. (43. 34-6.)

Mine [purpose] is to teach Men to despise death & to go on
In fearless majesty annihilating Self, laughing to scorn
Thy Laws & terrors, shaking down thy Synagogues as webs.
I come to discover before Heav'n & Hell the Self righteousness
In all its Hypocritic turpitude, opening to every eye

[1] *Vala*, 7a. 343-4. [2] *Jerusalem*, 42. 45. [3] Ibid. 8. 15, 16.
[4] *Milton*, 46. 35, 36. [5] *Jerusalem*, 41. 29, 30.

These wonders of Satan's holiness, shewing to the Earth
The Idol virtues of the Natural Heart, & Satan's Seat
Explore in all its Selfish Natural Virtue, & put off
In Self annihilation all that is not of God alone,
To put off Self & all I have, ever & ever. (43. 40–9.)

Man, then, can 'arise from Self by Self Annihilation',[1] and
there are four means by which this may be achieved. First, by
conscious acts of will; thus Blake spoke of 'willing sacrifice of
Self'.[2] Secondly, by self-examination:

To cleanse the Face of my Spirit by Self-examination,
To bathe in the Waters of Life, to wash off the Not Human,
I come in Self-annihilation & the grandeur of Inspiration.[3]

Thirdly, by the practice of mutual forgiveness: 'Forgiveness of
Sins which is Self Annihilation.'[4] And finally by the power of
Christ:

O Saviour pour upon me thy Spirit of meekness & love!
Annihilate the Selfhood in me: be thou all my life![5]

This death to self is a process, not an isolated act performed
once and for all, nor is it completed until that unity with God
is achieved in which 'thou . . . knowest not of self in thy supreme
joy',[6] and which is the goal of the mystic quest. 'This Union',
Blake declared after many years of earnest endeavour, 'was not
to be Effected without Cares & Sorrows & Troubles . . . of self
denial and of bitter Contrition.'[7] But with the initiation of this
dying, the condition of single vision is already beginning to pass
and entrance is being made into twofold vision, the neophyte's
foot being now firmly planted upon the first stage of the mystic
path.

Twofold vision is the condition of the man whose consciousness has been redirected from a self-centred world to a God-
centred world; it is in fact to be identified with that Illuminated
Life experienced by all true mystics, and shared to a greater or
less degree by all real artists. Its main feature is an increased
clarity of vision, so that 'everything appears to man as it is,
infinite', once 'the doors of perception' have been cleansed.[8]

---

[1] Ibid. 49. 45–6.
[2] Ibid. 28. 20.
[3] *Milton* 46. 37–48. 2.
[4] *Jerusalem*, 98. 23.
[5] Ibid. 5. 21, 22.
[6] Ibid. 12. 42.
[7] *Vala*, 7a. 397–9.
[8] *Marriage of Heaven and Hell*, p. 14.

This mystical illumination is especially enjoyed in regard to the world of nature; denying the artificial and narrow world of self, the mystic pierces through the veil of appearance and establishes direct contact with the heart of creation. 'Some things are little on the outside,' declared· Thomas Traherne, 'and rough and common, but I remember the time when the dust of the streets were as pleasing as Gold to my infant eyes'.

So Blake, who wrote of himself:

> double the vision my Eyes do see,
> And a double vision is always with me;[1]

made a new approach to nature, which led him to declare that 'Truth is Nature',[2] and that 'This World Is a World of Imagination & Vision . . . to the Eyes of the Man of Imagination, Nature is Imagination itself'.[3] 'Then tell me, what is the material world, and is it dead?' the poet asked his muse, in the rejected preface of *Europe*, and was told in reply:

> I'll sing to you to this soft lute, and shew you all alive
> The world, where every particle of dust breathes forth its joy.

The world then is not dead and, although encrusted with the illusions of matter which obscure the truth, it is eternal. Nature is indeed a 'Crystal house',[4] in which the stars 'reflect the Vision of beatitude',[5] and the trees are 'uttering prophecies & speaking instructive words to the sons Of men'.[6] But Blake was quick to give his warning against a relapse into single vision:

> These the Visions of Eternity,
> But we see only as it were the hem of their garments
> When with our vegetable eyes we view these wondrous Visions.[7]

'I question not my Corporeal or Vegetative Eye,' he affirmed, 'any more than I would Question a Window concerning a Sight. I look thro' it & not with it.'[8]

> This Life's dim Windows of the Soul
> Distorts the Heavens from Pole to Pole
> And leads you to Believe a Lie
> When you see with, not thro', the Eye,[9]

---

[1] *To Butts*, 22 Nov. 1802.
[2] M.D.P., pp. xviii–xix.
[3] *To Trusler*, 23 Aug. 1799.
[4] *Vala*, 9. 518.
[5] *Milton*, 27. 70.
[6] Ibid. 28. 9, 10.
[7] Ibid. 28. 10–12.
[8] *Last Judgment*, pp. 92–5.
[9] 'Everlasting Gospel', d. 98–101.

for the eye that has been hardened into material form 'is open all within And in this hallowed center holds the heavens of bright eternity'.[1] The difference between those who possess only single vision and those who have achieved twofold is exemplified by their attitude to the most common of natural objects. 'The tree which moves some to tears of joy is in the Eyes of others only a Green thing which stands in the way.'[2]

> A frowning Thistle implores my stay.
> What to other a trifle appears
> Fills me full of smiles or tears;
>
> .   .   .   .
>
> With my inward Eye 'tis an old Man grey;
> With my outward, a Thistle across my way.[3]

To Blake, with his illuminated vision, the world was transfigured; in this state of clarity, nature and imagination are seen to be one, a perception which he expressed so perfectly in the quatrain which begins the 'Auguries of Innocence':

> To see a World in a Grain of Sand
> And a Heaven in a Wild Flower,
> Hold Infinity in the palm of your hand
> And Eternity in an Hour.

'You never enjoy the world aright', said Traherne, 'till you see how a sand exhibiteth the wisdom and power of God.' Similarly Blake:

> every sand becomes a Gem
> Reflected in the beams divine.[4]

So close was Blake's communion with nature that he could look at a knot in a tree until it terrified him. This was not a form of self-hypnosis, as one critic considers, but the record of a genuine mystical experience. The tree had ceased to be an object to him and he had entered into a mutual relationship with it, encountering the very tree itself.

Blake believed that there was a way to eternity through nature.

> There is a Grain of Sand in Lambeth that Satan cannot find,
> Nor can his Watch Fiends find it; 'tis translucent.[5]

---

[1] *Milton*, 30. 37, 38.
[2] *To Trusler*, 23 Aug. 1799.
[3] *To Butts*, 22 Nov. 1802, 24–6, 29, 30.
[4] 'Mock on, Mock on'. . . .
[5] *Jerusalem*, 41. 15, 16.

For every Space larger than a red Globule of Man's blood
Is visionary . . .
And every Space smaller than a Globule of Man's blood opens
Into Eternity of which this vegetable Earth is but a shadow.[1]

Thou percievest the Flowers put forth their precious Odours,
And none can tell how from so small a center comes such sweets,
Forgetting that within that Center Eternity expands
Its ever during doors.[2]

Nature is indeed beautiful; to appreciate this we have only
to look at the lark whose 'every feather On throat & breast &
wings vibrates with the effluence Divine'.[3] But therein lies its
very danger, for this beauty may lure man into a too close
absorption in it. Whereas 'to learn the Language of Art, "Copy
for Ever" is My Rule',[4] nature merely teaches the alphabet of
painting, the rudiments of execution, which requires no great
study when once known. 'Models are difficult—enslave one
—efface from one's mind a conception or reminiscence which
was better.' The soul is born to aspiration and all the glory of
the heaven and the earth is about her, but this beauty will
enclose her and hold her in its toils unless she pierces through it
to the reality within.

Nature is to be valued, not only because of its beauty, but also
because it is a shadow of the eternal world. 'There Exist in that
Eternal World the Permanent Realities of Every Thing which
we see reflected in this Vegetable Glass of Nature',[5] that is,
natural things have their true being in 'the real & eternal World
of which this Vegetable Universe is but a faint shadow'.[6] 'The
outward world', wrote William Law, in similar vein, 'is but a
glass, or representation of the inward; and every thing and
variety of things in temporal nature must have its root, or
hidden cause, in something that is more inward.' This conception of type and anti-type was probably derived by Blake
from his own artistic experience, influenced by his reading of
Swedenborg. He painted from imagination; that is to say, his
paintings are representations of a pre-existent idea conceived
in the mind. The painting may be destroyed, but the idea
cannot thereby be obliterated; therefore, according to Blake,

[1] *Milton*, 31. 19–22.   [2] Ibid. 34. 46–9.
[3] Ibid. 34. 34, 35.   [4] *Reynolds*, Contents, Disc. 11.
[5] *Last Judgment*, pp. 69–70.   [6] *Jerusalem*, 77.

the idea is the reality, the painting only its shadow. By reveal-ing something of the idea through art, Blake was performing a religious work, imparting spiritual realities to others through the visual image; similarly, nature, seen by the man of illumi-nated vision, can convey to us something of the divine.

Blake's constant vacillation between the condemnation of the view of nature which is characteristic of single vision and his approval of the enlightened view of twofold vision serves to explain the apparent contradiction in his attitude to the world of phenomena. Nature beheld by the Imagination is reality itself; nature distorted by reason and the selfhood falls into the realm of non-entity. The visible universe is a symbol of the eternal; because it is not the eternal it is relatively unimportant; nevertheless because of what it symbolizes it has importance and significance. Hence the material world is unreal unless we see it as the artist sees it, with twofold vision; then it becomes an 'Image of regeneration';[1] then it becomes a way of return to eternity.

Illumination or twofold vision was the most constant feature of Blake's mysticism; he himself declared that it was 'twofold Always',[2] meaning thereby, not that he never ascended any higher, but that he never returned to the errors of single vision.

Threefold vision is the condition of the man who apprehends truth in a manner entirely supersensuous, by means of percep-tions which include the desires and higher aspirations of the soul. 'Man's perceptions are not bounded by organs of per-ception; he perceives more than sense (tho' ever so acute) can discover.'[3]

There are two extreme forms of contemplation, according to the mystic's predisposition to emphasize the transcendence or the immanence of God. In contemplating the transcendence, the mystic is aware of his own littleness and unworthiness, expresses his experience by negatives, and sees his communion with God as an entrance into a Divine Dark or Cloud of Un-knowing. In contemplating the immanence, the mystic is possessed by a sense of the nearness and intimacy of God, expresses his experience in terms of personality, and sees his communion with God as a marriage or a joyous and loving

---

[1] Ibid. 7. 65. [2] *To Butts*, 22 Nov. 1802, 87.
[3] *No Natural Religion*, ii. 1.

participation in the Divine Life. The one looks to the transcendent and unknowable Godhead, the other to the Incarnate Lord. Blake briefly outlined these two ways of approach when he wrote:

> God Appears & God is Light
> To those poor Souls who dwell in Night,
> But does a Human Form Display
> To those who Dwell in Realms of day.[1]

Blake himself was a mystic of the latter type, his creative genius allowed of no self-abasement, and his threefold vision is similar to that process of introversion by means of which the contemplative seeks union with the Godhead immanent within his own being. Hence the author of *De Adhaerando* says: 'To mount to God is to enter into one's self. For he who inwardly entereth and intimately penetrateth into himself, gets above and beyond himself and truly mounts up to God.' 'Let it be plainly understood', says St. Augustine, 'that we cannot return to God unless we enter first into ourselves. God is everywhere, but not everywhere to us. There is but one point in the Universe where God communicates with us, and that is the centre of our own soul. There He waits for us; there He meets us; there He speaks to us. To seek Him, therefore, we must enter into our own interior.'

Blake laid great emphasis on the immanence of God; an emphasis to which he was led, not only by his own temperament and preconceptions, but also by his antagonism to the remote Divine Being of the Deists. 'Seek not thy heavenly father then beyond the skies',[2] he admonished his readers; and in one passage he made Jesus say:

> I am not a God afar off, I am a brother & friend:
> Within your bosoms I reside, and you reside in me.[3]

God 'exists in us & we in him',[4] for 'what is Above is Within'.[5] So Blake was in the direct line of all those mystics who have laid stress upon the indwelling Godhead and with Brother Lawrence have asserted 'He is within us; seek Him not elsewhere.'

The method by which the contemplative penetrates within is

---

[1] 'Auguries of Innocence', 129–32. [2] *Milton*, 22. 32.
[3] *Jerusalem*, 4. 18, 19. [4] Berkeley, p. 219.
[5] *Jerusalem*, 71. 6.

known as introversion, which is not to be confounded with
introspection or mere self-examination. It is a turning inwards
to hold converse, not with oneself, but with the indwelling
Christ in the depths of the soul. To achieve this, according to
St. Augustine, 'the mind abstracts itself from all the bodily
senses, as interrupting it and confounding it with their din'.
Above all, it must free itself from the arrogant domination of
the discursive reason. Thus Pseudo-Dionysius counsels that 'in
the earnest exercise of mystic contemplation, thou leave the
senses and the activities of the intellect and all things that the
senses or the intellect can perceive', since 'by love may he
be gotten and holden, but by thought never'.[1] We see here a
close affinity with Blake's thought. 'The Reasoning Spectre',
he maintained, 'Stands between the Vegetative Man & his
Immortal Imagination.'[2] Hence his repudiation of reason, and
hence also his frequent rejection of nature on the grounds that
it tends to lure a man 'by her beauty outside of himself'.[3]

Once this negation of the senses and of reason has been
accomplished, a state of recollection ensues. Blake's powers of
recollection have been remarked upon by his friend J. T. Smith,
who said that he 'was supereminently endowed with the power
of disuniting all other thoughts from his mind, whenever he
wished to indulge in thinking of any particular subject'. In this
condition of quiet, the soul begins to be united with its 'ground'.
'Even I already feel a World within Opening its gates';[4] so
Blake describes the inception of this process, made possible
because
                    In your own Bosom you bear your Heaven
And Earth & all you behold; tho' it appears Without, it is Within.[5]
And every Human Vegetated Form in its inward recesses
Is a house of pleasantness & a garden of delight.[6]

Man, though withered into material form, is 'translucent all
within'.[7]

According to the mystics, the point of contact in the soul
between God and man is a Divine nucleus, variously called the
Spark, the Apex, or Synteresis. The origin of this belief is to be
traced to Tatian, who wrote 'in the beginning the spirit was a

---

[1] *Cloud of Unknowing*, chap. vi.   [2] *Jerusalem*, 36. 23, 24.
[3] Ibid. 86. 60.   [4] *Vala*, 7a. 363, 364.
[5] *Jerusalem*, 71. 17, 18.   [6] Ibid. 73. 48, 49.   [7] Ibid. 27, stanza 14.

constant companion of the soul, but forsook it because the soul
would not follow it; yet it retained, as it were, a spark of its
power'. From this starting-point it was a short step to the belief
that the divine element is not merely potential but actually
immanent, and so to the idea of deification. 'If', says Eckhart,
'I am to know God directly, I must become completely He and
He I: so that this He and this I become and are one.' The great
mystics safeguarded themselves against such extravagances. The
soul, so we are told by Louis of Blois, 'becomes one with God,
yet not so as to be of the same substance and nature as God'.
Blake, on the other hand, always prone to the most exaggerated
assertion of any truth he perceived, was guilty of many rash
and unqualified utterances. 'We are all co-existent with God,'
he told Crabb Robinson, 'members of the Divine body. We
are all partakers of the Divine nature.' The same source of
information tells us that 'on my asking in what light he viewed
the great question concerning the Divinity of Jesus Christ, he
said—"*He is the only God.*" But then he added—"And so am I
and so are you."' In making this affirmation Blake was
running counter to his master, Boehme, who with direct
simplicity says: 'even if Christ is born in us, nevertheless we
cannot say, in speaking of ourselves as a whole, "I am Christ",
for the external man is not Christ. We can only say honestly,
"I am in Christ, and Christ has become human in me."'

The birth of Christ in the soul is an idea more or less taught
and accepted by all those mystics of the immanental type.
Whereas for traditional Christianity the Incarnation is synonymous with the historical birth of Jesus, for them it is not only
that but also a continual personal process. 'The one secret, the
greatest of all,' says Coventry Patmore, is 'the doctrine of the
Incarnation, regarded not as an historical event which occurred
two thousand years ago, but as an event which is renewed in
the body of every one who is in the way to the fulfilment of his
original destiny.' So the mystics see the life of Christ in history
as the pattern or epitome of all spiritual life, which every soul
striving for union with God must experience. If one asks how
this birth in the soul is to be effected, how this process is to be
initiated, the answer lies in the doctrine of the synteresis. 'The
Saviour of the world,' wrote William Law, 'the eternal Word of
God lies hid in thee, as a spark of the divine nature which is to

overcome sin and death and hell within thee, and generate the life of Heaven again in thy soul. Turn to thy heart, and thy heart will find its Saviour, its God within itself.'

The mystics pass easily from the Christ of the Gospels to the Eternal Christ; this is not a disparagement of history, it is their tribute to its eternal value, for they see in the present 'a vision of the Eternal Now'.[1]

Many writers are of the opinion that Blake interpreted the doctrine of the Incarnation as entirely an inward occurrence, and attributed little importance to it as an historical event. This is almost certainly incorrect; Blake's belief, as we shall see, was quite orthodox. However, in company with his fellow mystics, he did on occasion consider the birth of Jesus as a personal process, as an influx of spiritual light, that is, of Imagination, 'which is the Divine Body of the Lord Jesus'.[2]

We may conclude by saying that threefold vision is the state of the man who has passed beyond reasoning and inquiry into a condition of repose and peaceful communion with God. It is therefore associated with the Quietists. It is a refuge or *ne plus ultra* for those who are incapable of attaining to the highest vision; as such, it is imperfect; hence in so far as it is above single vision and double vision it is to be valued, but in so far as it is below fourfold vision it lacks completeness and by comparison may even be said to be false.

Fourfold vision is that state to which all mystics aspire, the condition of complete union with God, or in Blake's own words: 'With holy raptures of adoration, rap'd sublime in the Visions of God.'[3] This is achieved when 'Self was lost in the contemplation of faith And wonder at the Divine Mercy'.[4] Its attainment is rare in this life, but Blake had had experience of it:

> Now I a fourfold vision see,
> And a fourfold vision is given to me;
> 'Tis fourfold in my supreme delight.[5]

This climax is only once described:

> Terror-struck in the Vale I stood at that immortal sound.
> My bones trembled, I fell outstretch'd upon the path
> A moment, & my Soul return'd into its mortal State.[6]

---

[1] Lavater, 407. [2] *Milton*, 3. 3, 4. [3] *Jerusalem*, 79. 44.
[4] Ibid. 96. 31, 32. [5] *To Butts*, 22 Nov. 1802, 83–5. [6] *Milton*, 49. 24–6.

Blake usually expressed the activities of the perfect visionary state under the symbols of mental and spiritual warfare and hunting. Thus he spoke of 'the two Sources of Life in Eternity, Hunting and War',[1] and of 'War & Hunting, the Two Fountains of the River of Life'.[2] This spiritual warfare is to be contrasted with corporeal strife,

> Our wars are wars of life, & wounds of love
> With intellectual spears, & long winged arrows of thought.[3]

'I will not cease from Mental Fight',[4] he declared, affirming that he was engaged in 'the great Wars of Eternity, in fury of Poetic Inspirations.'[5] This imagery, acceptable to Blake because of his insistence on the active life, was probably derived from Boehme: 'Man must here be at war with himself if he wishes to be a heavenly citizen . . . fighting must be the watchword, not with tongue and sword, but with mind and spirit; and not to give over.'

The psychological state of the man who is in 'Immediate Communion with God'[6] would appear to be something akin to a condition between waking and sleeping. This is achieved when his four basic psychological functions, which in the natural man are habitually opposed, are in harmony, as in moments of inspiration. But the distinction between this synthesis, this 'Divine Union' of fourfold vision, and threefold vision is lacking in clarity. The difference would seem to lie in the fact that by means of the lower type of vision a man may convey a divine message and so reveal the nature of the Real; whereas the visionary of the highest type becomes 'a conscious element of the Ideal, and enjoys the experience of immediately apprehending the homogeneity of all Being in Time and in Eternity',[7] so that 'the Divine Vision remains Every-where For-ever'.[8]

It will be noticed that, in the foregoing account of the contemplative's progress, no mention has been made of the Dark Night of the Soul which is such a constant feature in the experience of the great mystics. It is characterized by a conviction of abandonment by God, by an emotional lassitude, and by a stagnation of the will and intelligence, all of which are accompanied by a feeling of impotence and distress. These

---

[1] *Jerusalem*, 43. 31.   [2] *Milton*, 39. 2.   [3] *Jerusalem*, 38. 14, 15.
[4] *Milton*, preface.   [5] Ibid. 33. 19.   [6] Laocoon.
[7] Sloss and Wallis, op. cit., vol. ii, p. 39.   [8] *Milton*, 24. 2.

combine to effect a final purification of the soul that it may be
united without reserve with God. Although Foster Damon
considers that Blake underwent this experience during the
years 1794 and 1795, and Maung Ba-Han is of the opinion that
he had two such periods, this is far from certain, and indeed
there seems to be no place for it in Blake's scheme. However,
there is some indication that he was not a stranger to this condition although, in the same way that the difference between
threefold and fourfold vision is not made plain, so the exact
nature of Blake's Dark Night of the Soul is not clear, and it may
be that it was nothing more than a phase of acute depression.
In a letter to Thomas Butts,[1] Blake wrote: 'Temptations are on
the right hand & left; behind, the sea of time & space roars &
follows swiftly; he who keeps not right onward is lost, & if our
footsteps slide in clay, how can we do otherwise than fear &
tremble?' This seems to indicate some kind of spiritual crisis,
but not of any long duration, as he continued towards the end
of the same letter, 'But I am now no longer in That State, &
now go on again with my Task, Fearless, and tho' my path is
difficult, I have no fear of stumbling while I keep it.' Two years
later, reporting his progress to Hayley in obtaining information
for his former patron's life of Romney, he wrote: 'Suddenly, on
the day after visiting the Truchsessian Gallery of pictures, I was
again enlightened with the light I enjoyed in my youth, and
which has for exactly twenty years been closed from me as by
a door and by window-shutters'; and later 'I am really drunk
with intellectual vision whenever I take a pencil or graver into
my hand, even as I used to be in my youth, and as I have not
been for twenty dark, but very profitable, years. I thank God
that I courageously pursued my course through darkness.'[2]
But the way was still fraught with difficulty, and three years
after this last statement we meet this brief memorandum:
'Tuesday, Janry. 20, 1807, between Two & Seven in the
Evening—Despair.' This is the sum total of the evidence at our
disposal, and it is palpably insufficient to warrant any final
conclusion or dogmatic assertion.[3]

[1] 10 Jan. 1802.
[2] 23 Oct. 1804.
[3] According to E. H. Short (*Blake*, 1925, p. 112) Blake's picture of the Crucifixion (*Jerusalem*, 76) is a representation of the Dark Night of the Soul; but this
interpretation, while not impossible, has nothing to support it.

Although the works of the contemplatives are more widely known at the present day, mysticism is still generally regarded as an esoteric form of devotion, to which few are called and in which fewer succeed. But this belief is contrary to the teaching of the great mystics, who maintained that contemplation was open to all. 'Some of the least ones, who yet perseveringly walk in the path of faith, come to that most blessed contemplation', wrote St. Augustine, and St. Gregory's exposition of the contemplative life was not given to the select circle of his monks but in public sermons to mixed congregations. 'There is no state of life of the faithful', he asserted, 'from which the grace of contemplation can be excluded.' That this was Blake's view is evident from Crabb Robinson's report: 'Of the faculty of Vision, he spoke as one he had had from early infancy. He thinks all men partake of it, but it is lost by not being cultivated.' To this faculty Blake gave the name Emanation.

The Emanation is the visionary capacity in men, the means of achieving the highest unity. Hence he wrote of 'the Mystic Union of the Emanation in the Lord'.[1] It stands in opposition to the disintegrating physical perception (the Shadow), and to attain the heights of contemplation it must be free from interference by the reason (the Spectre). With similar but more extended meaning Blake used the term Imagination, 'Imagination, which is Spiritual Sensation.'[2] 'Imagination is the Divine Vision not of The World, or of Man, nor from Man as he is a Natural Man, but only as he is a Spiritual Man';[3]—'the Human Imagination, which is the Divine Vision & Fruition In which Man liveth eternally.'[4] So Blake could affirm 'The Imaginative Image returns by the seed of Contemplative Thought'.[5] 'One Power alone makes a poet': he believed, 'Imagination, The Divine Vision'.[6] The step from this to identifying the Imagination with Inspiration is a short one. 'Imagination is surrounded by the daughters of Inspiration.'[7] Further 'it is the gift of God, it is inspiration and vision. . . . The human mind cannot go beyond the gift of God, the Holy Ghost.'[8] It is therefore the means of penetrating through the

[1] *Jerusalem*, 53. 24.
[2] *To Trusler*, 23 Aug. 1799.
[3] Wordsworth, pp. 374–5.
[4] *Milton*, 35. 19, 20.
[5] *Last Judgment*, pp. 68, 69.
[6] Wordsworth, p. viii.
[7] *Last Judgment*, p. 68.
[8] *Descriptive Catalogue*, v.

temporal to the eternal. 'This world of Imagination is the world of Eternity. . . . This World of Imagination is Infinite & Eternal, whereas the world of Generation, or Vegetation, is Finite & Temporal. There Exist in that Eternal World the Permanent Realities of Every Thing which we see reflected in this Vegetable Glass of Nature.'[1] Men fail to realize this because 'the Nature of Visionary Fancy, or Imagination, is very little known, & the Eternal nature & permanence of its ever Existent Images is consider'd as less permanent than the things of Vegetative & Generative Nature; yet the Oak dies as well as the Lettuce, but Its Eternal Image & Individuality never dies, but renews by its seed',[2] that is to say, of any natural object 'its Reality is its Imaginative Form',[3] 'For all Things Exist in the Human Imagination';[4] 'Imagination, the real & eternal World of which this Vegetable Universe is but a faint shadow, & in which we shall live in our Eternal or Imaginative Bodies when these Vegetable Mortal Bodies are no more.'[5] But Blake was not content to rest here, and proceeded to identify Imagination with the Divine Image on the grounds that 'Jesus considered Imagination to be that Real Man',[6] and therefore 'Imagination is the Divine Body in Every Man',[7] i.e. 'Imagination or the Human Eternal Body in Every Man'.[8] His final conclusion was that Imagination is the 'Divine Body of the Lord Jesus',[9] or the 'Divine-Humanity'[10] or the 'Bosom of God'.[11]

The great enemy of this vision is nature wrongly perceived, and Blake laid great stress on the definiteness that distinguishes imaginative vision from that of the senses:

> with bounds to the Infinite putting off the Indefinite
> Into most holy forms of Thought; such is the power of inspiration,[12]

and, we may add, of Imagination. 'Nature has no Outline, but Imagination has.'[13] Hence his condemnation of Dante on the grounds that 'Nature is his Inspirer & not . . . the Holy Ghost'.[14] Therefore 'Imagination has nothing to do with memory'. It is

[1] *Last Judgment*, pp. 69, 70.
[2] Ibid., pp. 68, 69.
[3] Berkeley, p. 213.
[4] *Jerusalem*, 69. 25.
[5] Ibid. 77.
[6] Berkeley, p. 212.
[7] Ibid., p. 204.
[8] Ibid., p. 203.
[9] *Milton*, 3. 4.
[10] *Jerusalem*, 70. 19, 20.
[11] Ibid. 5. 20.
[12] *Milton*, 30. 4, 5.
[13] *Ghost of Abel*.
[14] Notes on Ill. to Dante.

immediate perception of truth given by God. 'I know what is
true by internal conviction,' he remarked to the painstaking
diarist.

Blake believed that all men might approach God, and the task
he set himself was

> To open the Eternal Worlds, to open the immortal Eyes
> Of Man inwards into the Worlds of Thought, into Eternity
> Ever expanding in the Bosom of God, the Human Imagination.[1]

Blake's desire that all men should in some degree embrace the
mystic life did not lead him to expect a diminution of activity
among those who answered his call; on the contrary, in company
with the great contemplatives he envisaged a life of far greater
intensity than before. 'In contemplation,' writes Ruysbroeck,
'God comes to us without ceasing and demands of us both
action and fruition, in such a way that the one never impedes
but always strengthens the other. And therefore the most
inward man lives his life in these two ways, namely, in work and
in rest.' So Blake revealed that

> There is a Moment in each Day that Satan cannot find,
> Nor can his Watch Fiends find it; but the Industrious find
> This Moment & it multiply, & when it once is found
> It renovates every Moment of the Day if rightly placed.[2]

Blake's constant alternation between prayer and work is de-
lightfully illustrated by the anecdote preserved by Gilchrist of
the young artist who 'finding his invention flag' came to Blake
for comfort and advice. Blake turned to his wife and said: 'It
is just so with us, is it not, for weeks together, when the visions
forsake us? What do we do then, Kate?' 'We kneel down and
pray, Mr. Blake.'

Blake's visions are a most important factor in evaluating his
mysticism, for the majority of the great contemplatives dis-
parage and discourage them. 'Fly from them,' advises St. John
of the Cross, 'without seeking to know whether their origin be
good or evil,' and Mme Guyon warns us that it is 'of great
importance to prevent souls from relying upon visions and
ecstasies, because this retards them almost all their life'. Blake,
on the other hand, deliberately cultivated them, being sent

---

[1] *Jerusalem*, 5. 18–20.   [2] *Milton*, 39. 42–5.

'a-screaming' by his first at the age of four, and in his advanced years calmly sketching their portraits into the early hours of the morning, in the company of John Varley, the water-colourist. Because of this attitude of Blake, several critics are of the opinion that as a mystic he cannot be rated highly. But however the leading contemplatives may have condemned such modes of revelation 'it is not too much to say, indeed, that most, if not all, of their most fruitful and dynamic intuitions and their most influential and redemptive activities were inspired by psychic experiences'.[1] They realized acutely the dangers of pride and self-deception to which visions might give rise, but such experiences were often the vehicles of their deepest understanding of the Eternal. Therefore, although Blake did not share their rejection of these experiences, he did share their discernment of them and admitted openly what they, in practice, avowed, namely, the validity of visions as a means of acquiring supersensual knowledge. 'Can a Poet doubt the Visions of Jehovah?'[2] asked Blake, 'were it not better to believe Vision With all our might & strength, tho' we are fallen & lost?'[2] 'Inspiration & Vision was then, & now is, & I hope will always Remain, my Element, my Eternal Dwelling place.'[3]

The question of the objectivity of Blake's visions need not concern us, nor is it of importance; their validity does not depend upon their objectivity, but upon their practical effects upon his life and thought; and the vigour of his life and the genius of his painting give ample proof of their fruition. However, mention may be made of his cool sanity in discussing them. 'When he said *my visions*,' reports the faithful, if sometimes inaccurate, Crabb Robinson, 'it was in the ordinary unemphatic tone in which we speak of trivial matters that every one understands and cares nothing about.' So on the occasion when Rudall, the flautist, called upon him 'the mystic told his visitor that he had a palace of his own of great beauty and magnificence. On Mr. Rudall's looking round the room for evidence, Blake remarked, "You don't think I'm such a fool as to think this is it?" '

The visions of an artist are not necessarily of the same nature as those of a contemplative; with the former these psychic

---

[1] E. Herman, *The Meaning and Value of Mysticism*, 1922, p. 54.
[2] *Ghost of Abel.*　　　　　　　　　[3] Reynolds, p. 244.

experiences expend themselves in creative work, with the latter they issue in a transformation of personality. As Blake's art was the practical expression of his mysticism, his aesthetic problems were religious problems; and so, for example, the painters of the Venetian and Flemish schools, in whose work light and shade are such prominent features, became 'Demons' in Blake's eyes, 'labouring to destroy Imaginative power, by means of that infernal machine called Chiaro Oscuro'.[1] Again 'the spirit of Titian was particularly active in raising doubts concerning the possibility of executing without a model, and when once he had raised the doubt, it became easy for him to snatch away the vision time after time'.[1] Even Blake's attitude to nature, which seems essentially that of a mystic, is inseparable from his artistic ideas. 'We are in a World of Generation & death, & this world we must cast off', he said, in words which express clearly the mystic path of Detachment, but then he continued 'if we would be Painters such as Rafael, Mich. Angelo & the Ancient Sculptors; if we do not cast off this world we shall only be Venetian Painters, who will be cast off & Lost from Art.'[2] Hence his experience after his visit to the Truchsessian Gallery may probably have had artistic implications, and the 'spectrous fiend' may well have been Chiaro Oscuro or some other problem of colouring or execution that was exercising his mind at that period.

Blake was, indeed, a mystic; although this has been denied, but on insufficient grounds. Blake's mysticism is self-evident, and it has been accepted by the majority of his critics as the key to his personality and beliefs; yet they also concur in the judgement that he was one who never gained the heights of mystical experience, that his mysticism was potential and never realized.

The elements in Blake's mysticism which have led to this conclusion may be briefly enumerated. In the first place, it is contended that he practised no asceticism; but, as we have seen, this is not an essential component of mysticism and, although Blake may not have been a saint, he was certainly a mystic. Secondly, it is maintained that prayer and meditation had no part in his system; but while Blake has left no detailed account

[1] *Descriptive Catalogue*, ix.
[2] *Last Judgment*, pp. 90, 91.

of his prayer life, it is undeniable that he was a man of prayer. What could be more devotional than this cry from the heart?

> O how can I with my gross tongue that cleaveth to the dust
> Tell of the Four-fold Man in starry numbers fitly order'd,
> Or how can I with my cold hands of clay! But thou, O Lord,
> Do with me as thou wilt! for I am nothing, and vanity.[1]

Thirdly, his reliance on visions is said to be a sign of immature contemplation; here, again, as we have seen, Blake was only making open declaration of what the great mystics tacitly assumed and from which they derived their sublimest perceptions of truth. Finally, Blake is said to have been lacking in humility and to have displayed personal animus in his work which is inconsistent with true mysticism. As will be made evident when his ethics are reviewed, Blake, while repudiating humility in the sense of that false abasement that denies the operation of the Holy Spirit in man, stoutly affirmed the true Christian doctrine of humility which thinks nothing of self but only of God. On the other hand, it is true that Blake did display a certain acerbity in his works, but it must be remembered that hatred of all that is evil should be natural to the Christian character, and Blake's bitterness was seldom directed against individuals as such, but against the false ideas they propounded; his doctrine of states and his insistence on the need for continual forgiveness serve only as means to explain the dictum 'Condemn the sin, but not the sinner'.[2] His generous spirit, even towards those who he deemed had wronged him, is shown by his attempts to be reconciled with Stothard, in which he persisted even after his first harsh rebuff. 'They pity me,' he said of his detractors, 'but 'tis they are the just objects of pity: I possess my visions and peace. They have bartered their birthright for a mess of pottage.'

The marks of the true mystic, according to Miss Underhill, are fourfold. First, he must be practical, not theoretical; that Blake was such there can be no denial; on the contrary, the understanding of his mysticism would have been much facili-

---

[1] *Milton*, 22. 15–18.
[2] Yet Blake was not a saint, even though he was a mystic, and he did not always manage to practise what he preached; thus his attitude to Cromek was certainly that of an embittered individual, and not, it may be added, without considerable provocation.

tated if he had only given more exposition. Secondly, he must live for God alone and not for self; Blake's strenuous and unremitting efforts to annihilate his selfhood and his utter detachment from material things, joined to his personal devotion to Jesus, show certainly that this was characteristic of him. Thirdly, his life must reveal increased fervour and love. 'I cry: Love! Love! Love!' sang Blake, 'happy, happy Love! free as the mountain wind!'[1]

> Seek love in the Pity of others' Woe,
> In the gentle relief of another's care,
> In the darkness of night & the winter's snow,
> In the naked & outcast, Seek Love there![2]

Lastly, he must pursue the mystic way, impelled by an ardent desire for God and a thirst for moral perfection. Blake's ardent desire for God is unquestionable, but he had no thirst for moral perfection. It is true that he had a sense of sin—'I am perhaps the most sinful of men. I pretend not to holiness: yet I pretend to love, to see, to converse with daily as man with man, & the more to have an interest in the Friend of Sinners'[3]—but it was not this that led him along the path of mysticism, it was his creative genius, and 'Creation is in a profound sense the contemplation of God, truth, and beauty, or the supreme life of the spirit. God is not content that man should seek salvation, for He wants man to reveal his creative love for Himself in the positive revelation of his nature.'[4] Creativeness involves an asceticism of its own, which is different in kind from that connected with traditional mysticism; the artist is purified, but not by feats of self-abnegation, rather by the trials of life itself, and 'these souls, whose style of life is active, will have the grace of contemplation, but of a masked, unapparent contemplation'.[5]

> I am in God's presence night & day,
> And he never turns his face away.[6]

Christianity, although having affinities with other religions, is totally distinct from them, and the very factors which contribute to this distinction make of it the ideal setting for the mystic

---

[1] *Daughters of Albion*, 191.   [2] 'William Bond', stanza 13.
[3] *Jerusalem*, 3.
[4] Berdyaev, *Freedom and the Spirit*, p. 232.
[5] J. Maritain, *Questions de conscience*, Paris, essay 'Action et contemplation', p. 152.
[6] 'I rose up at the dawn of day.'

life. 'Its note of close intimacy, of direct and personal contact with a spiritual reality given here and now—its astonishing combination of splendour and simplicity, of the sacramental and transcendent—all these things minister to the needs of the mystical type. Hence the Christian system, or some colourable imitation of it, has been found essential by almost all the great mystics of the West.'[1] So with Blake, the greater his inspiration, the more forcible his utterances, 'the more passionately and dogmatically Christian even this hater of the Churches becomes'.[1]

[1] Underhill, op. cit., p. 106.

V

HIS DOCTRINE OF GOD

THE elucidation of Blake's doctrine of God is usually rendered difficult, if not impossible, by a misunderstanding of the extent to which he ascribed objective reality to the mythological figures which people his Prophetic books. Most critics have assumed, without due consideration, that these beings are not mere personifications, but are actually spiritual agents possessing an existence of their own, distinct from the poems and from the mind of their creator. Further confusion has been introduced into the subject by the attribution of objective existence to some, while at the same time the rest are dismissed as symbols of psychological states. Thus one writer can maintain that Blake was a Gnostic, his 'Urizen' being the demiurge, and his 'Eternals' the Aeons; but it is difficult to see how this can be reconciled with the statement, also by the same author, albeit in a later book, that 'all the terrible Shades of the Prophecies, Urizen and Los, and *Vala* and *Enitharmon* are only expressions of parts of Blake's mind and thought; and the subject of all his poems is the description of the passionate conflicts raging perpetually in his own wild and populous soul'.[1] It is surely evident that Blake's characters have to be conceived either all ontologically or all symbolically; there can be no intermediate position.

Blake himself provided the key to the true interpretation of his works. Writing in answer to an inquiring patron, he listed *America, Europe, Visions of the Daughters of Albion, Urizen,* and *Milton,* and said that these poems consisted of 'Poetical Personifications & Acts'.[2] Indeed, to affirm the objective reality of his creations is 'to turn allegoric and mental signification into corporeal command';[3] and to 'abstract the mental deities from their objects',[4] thus 'choosing forms of worship from poetic tales'.[4] Blake had no doubts about this; 'these

---

[1] D. Saurat, *Blake and Modern Thought,* 1929, pp. 12, 91–7; *Blake and Milton,* 1935, p. 18.
[2] *To Dawson Turner,* 9 June 1818.   [3] *Descriptive Catalogue,* v.
[4] *Marriage of Heaven and Hell,* p. 11.

gods', he said, 'are visions of the eternal attributes, or divine names, which, when erected into gods, become destructive to humanity';[1] they are 'Qualities, which are Servants of Humanity, not Gods or Lords'.[2] The characters themselves admit that

> in the Brain of Man we live & in his circling Nerves,
> . . . . . this bright world of all our joy is in the Human Brain.[3]

Blake's mythological figures then are mental relationships, dispositions of the soul or psychological diagrams.[4] He was in effect a mystic of the subjective and personal type, and his prophetic books are mainly symbolic dissertations on the psychology of the soul.

The conclusion that these beings cannot be taken into account in considering Blake's doctrine of God does not necessarily involve a denial of his supposed Gnosticism. On the contrary, Crabb Robinson would lead one to imagine that there can be no doubt of it, for he summarized part of a conversation with Blake as 'the doctrine of the Gnostics repeated with sufficient consistency to silence one so unlearned as myself'. This assertion would seem to derive support from Blake's frequent references to the 'Selfish father of men',[5] the 'Father of Jealousy',[6] who is 'the God of This World'.[7] But a close reading of Blake's works, which are always more to be relied upon than reports of his conversation, suggests that Crabb Robinson's account cannot be accepted, and that rather, on that occasion, the prosaic and unimaginative diarist misunderstood what was being said to him. This being would appear to be the metaphysical god of the Deists, the 'God who dwells in Chaos hidden from the human sight.'[8] They professed to believe in a god who

> in the dreary Void
> Dwells from Eternity, wide separated from the Human Soul.[9]

But Blake considered this 'god' a mere abstraction, to whom he referred as a 'Demon of smoke', and 'this abstract non-entity'.[10]

[1] Descriptive Catalogue, 111.
[2] Milton, 35. 21.　　　　　　　　　　　　　[3] Vala, 1. 294, 295.
[4] Cf. L. A. Duncan-Johnstone, A Psychological Study of William Blake, 1945, and W. P. Witcutt, Blake, A Psychological Study, 1946.
[5] 'Earth's Answer', stanza 2.　　　　　　　[6] 'To Nobodaddy.'
[7] Gates of Paradise, epilogue.　　　　　　　[8] Jerusalem, 28. 16.
[9] Ibid. 23. 29, 30.　　　　　　　　　　　　[10] Ahania, 1. 2.

'There is a God of this World', he said, but he is 'A God Worship'd in this World as God & set above all that is call'd God'.[1] In other words, Blake maintained that many of his contemporaries, and especially those who called themselves Deists, worshipped a being whom they addressed as 'God', who was in fact the product of their own reason and had no existence in reality; he was 'Nobodaddy'.

Sometimes this 'God' is called Satan:

> Satan, making to himself Laws from his own identity,
> Compell'd others to serve him in moral gratitude & submission,
> Being call'd God, setting himself above all that is called God;
> And all the Spectres of the Dead, calling themselves Sons of God,
> In his Synagogues worship Satan under the Unutterable Name.[2]

Man must & will have Some Religion: if he has not the Religion of Jesus, he will have the Religion of Satan . . . calling the Prince of this World, God, and destroying all who do not worship Satan under the Name of God. Will any one say, 'Where are those who worship Satan under the Name of God?' Where are they? Listen! Every Religion that Preaches Vengeance for Sin is the Religion of the Enemy & Avenger and not of the Forgiver of Sin, and their God is Satan, Named by the Divine Name. Your Religion, O Deists! Deism, is the Worship of the God of this World.[3]

In view of these passages the problem of the existence of this 'God' presents itself again. According to Crabb Robinson, Blake 'asserted that the Devil is eternally created not by God, but by God's permission'. It is possible to interpret this statement as meaning that Satan is a self-existent being, though inferior to God, and so the charge of Gnosticism seems justified after all. But Blake employed the term Satan in several ways. At one time it is a symbol of the aggregate of evil men—'men in union blasphemous Against the Divine image'.[4] At another it is the name of a state through which mankind passes in the process of regeneration. Finally, it is used to represent the degree of evil permitted by God before that process began.[5] It is this last connotation that illuminates Blake's remark to Crabb Robinson, indicating that his meaning was that God

---

[1] Watson, p. 35.   [2] Milton, 12. 10–14.
[3] Jerusalem, 52.
[4] Vala, 8. 255, 256.
[5] Jerusalem, 35. 1, 2; 42. 29–31.

did not create evil, but that it exists by His permission and is
made by Him to subserve the ends of redemption.

> Tho' thou art Worship'd by the Names Divine
> Of Jesus & Jehovah, thou art still
> The Son of Morn in weary Night's decline,
> The Lost Traveller's Dream under the Hill.[1]

Hence whether the 'God of this world' is taken to mean the
Deist abstraction or Satan, neither is a demiurge and neither
gives grounds for attributing Gnostic doctrines to Blake.[2]

Blake then was a monotheist; God is the source of all being,
the One 'who only Is'.[3] 'There is but one Omnipotent, Un-
create & God.'[4] He is a Personal Being, for 'he, who adores an
impersonal God, has none; and without guide or rudder,
launches on an immense abyss that first absorbs his powers, and
next himself'.[5] Hence God is called the Father of all mankind.
'I see the face of my Heavenly Father,' wrote Blake to Butts,
'he lays his Hand upon my Head & gives a blessing to all my
works.'[6] By His providence He directs mankind, His design
being to cast out error, and to bring all created beings into
spiritual communion with Himself. 'The Lord our father will
do for us & with us according to his divine will for our Good.'[7]
This is not a declaration of God's predestination nor a denial
of man's free will; man is

By Providence Divine conducted—not bent from his own will
Lest Death Eternal should be the result, for the Will cannot be
    violated.[8]

'The Will', affirmed Blake, 'must not be bended but in the day
of Divine Power.'[9] But God 'loves the lowly',[10] and 'all things
are so constructed And builded by the Divine hand that the
sinner shall always escape'.[11]

---

[1] Gates of Paradise, epilogue.
[2] We may note here that Blake's ideas as a whole had no affinity with those of
Gnosticism. His 'emanations' are totally unlike those of the Valentinians, and the
process of creation, according to him, was quite different; nor did he believe, like
the Marcionites, in several distinct and independent principles.
[3] Jerusalem, 55. 17.   [4] M.D.L.W., p. 24.   [5] Lavater, 552.
[6] 25 Apr. 1803.   [7] To Flaxman, 21 Sept. 1800.   [8] Vala, 6. 282–3.
[9] Jerusalem, 44. 18, 19.   [10] Thel, iii. 13.
[11] Jerusalem, 31. 30, 31. Blake did not reconcile grace and free will, but here
a possible solution is adumbrated, viz. that there is a providence that makes men's
actions produce the experiences necessary to purge their errors.

God is omnipotent,[1] but His power is limited in two ways: first by man's free will, and second by the fact that He cannot do anything that is self-contradictory, 'No Omnipotence can act against order'.[2] Further, He is omnipresent:

> For whether they look'd upward they saw the Divine Vision,
> Or whether they look'd downward still they saw the Divine Vision
> Surrounding them on all sides.[3]

'The Divine Vision', declared Blake, 'remains Every-where For-ever',[4] and elsewhere he asserted that 'God is in the lowest effects as well as in the highest causes'.[5] Above all, 'God is Love',[6] and therefore He is also infinite, that is eternal, for 'if a thing loves it is infinite'.[7] But in this He is not alone: 'That there is but one Infinite I do not (agree); for if all but God is not Infinite, they shall come to an End, which God forbid.'[8] Blake thus safeguarded the truth that man was created an 'image of the Eternal Father',[9] and as such is a partaker of the divine life of the spirit, for 'every thing on earth is the word of God & in its essence is God'.[10] To affirm that God is infinite is not to dissipate His Personality in a boundless abyss, for 'the Infinite alone resides in Definite & Determinate Identity'.[11]

God alone is holy, but He cannot be called good, for He is beyond good and evil and is *coincidentia oppositorum*. In His eyes no one is pure, not even the angels in heaven. Nevertheless He is liable to error. 'Did he not repent him that he had made Nineveh?' he asked Crabb Robinson. This idea is an echo of Milton's thought:

> Evil into the mind of God or man
> May come and go.

But this is only possible because God is the One and all is in Him. The whole of life is the procession of the Many out of the One, and their inclination back to the One, and so all discords are resolved when considered as parts of the universal harmony.

---

[1] According to Crabb Robinson, Blake denied God's omnipotence. Blake was either contradicting himself or possibly he meant that God's omnipotence cannot contradict itself.

[2] Lavater, 426.

[3] *Vala*, 8. 47–9.

[4] *Milton*, 24. 2.

[5] Lavater, 630.

[6] *Jerusalem*, 96. 27.

[7] M.D.L.W., p. 40.

[8] Ibid., p. 24.

[9] *Vala*, 9. 642.

[10] Lavater, 630.

[11] *Jerusalem*, 55. 64.

On this principle, Blake could assert that there is suffering in heaven, for where there is the capacity for enjoyment there is the capacity for pain. So he believed in

> the Divine Lord & Saviour, who suffers with those that suffer;
> For not one sparrow can suffer & the whole Universe not suffer also
> In all its Regions, & its Father & Saviour not pity and weep.[1]

Knowledge of the Godhead is possible because God is immanent in humanity. The inner Being of God we cannot know; all the knowledge we can possess is limited to what He is to us and in us. Hence Blake declared 'It is the God in *all* that is our companion & friend, for our God himself says: "you are my brother, my sister, & my mother," & St. John: "Whoso dwelleth in love dwelleth in God & God in him".'[2] So 'What is Above is Within',[3] and God proclaims:

> I am not a God afar off, I am a brother and friend:
> Within your bosoms I reside, and you reside in me.[4]

> Why stand we here trembling around
> Calling on God for help, and not ourselves, in whom God dwells?[5]

If Blake had gone no farther, his orthodoxy on this point would never have been held in question, but other and more extreme statements have given rise to the charge of pantheism. 'Those who envy or calumniate great men hate God, for there is no other God.'[6] 'God only Acts & Is, in existing beings or Men.'[7] These affirmations present a problem which must be solved before Blake's doctrine of God can be made finally clear; the problem being that they seem to contradict what he had to say elsewhere. Their obvious meaning seems to be that God is nothing more than man, and as such they have been interpreted by many of Blake's critics. But in other passages Blake made it plain that, while emphasizing the immanence of God, he did not lose the transcendence. 'God is within & without: he is even in the depths of Hell!'[8] In so far then as He is 'without' He cannot be exclusively innate in man whom He must in some measure transcend. Blake repeatedly spoke of God as a Being

---

[1] *Jerusalem*, 25. 7–9.   [2] Lavater, 630.
[3] *Jerusalem*, 71. 6.   [4] Ibid. 4. 18, 19.
[5] Ibid. 43. 12, 13.   [6] *Marriage of Heaven and Hell*, p. 23.
[7] Ibid., p. 16.   [8] *Jerusalem*, 12. 15.

who is above man and distinct from him, but Who of His mercy
comes and dwells in and with man.

>   And this is the Covenant
>   Of Jehovah: if you Forgive one-another, so shall Jehovah Forgive
>   You,
>   That He Himself may Dwell among You.[1]

'The Ancients did not mean to Impose when they affirm'd their
belief in Vision & Revelation. Plato was in Earnest: Milton
was in Earnest. They believ'd that God did Visit Man Really
& Truly.'[2] Although 'we are all co-existent with God—
members of the Divine body', and although 'we are partakers
of the Divine Nature', yet God is, apart from man whom He
transcends, and in whom He is immanent. But even this
immanence has its degrees: 'I have the happiness of seeing the
Divine Countenance in such men as Cowper & Milton more
distinctly than in any prince or hero.'[3] If, however, Blake
taught the true Christian doctrine of God's 'otherness' and
nearness to man, what interpretation is to be given to those
pronouncements quoted above which suggest pantheistic
leanings? It is possible to consider them from two points of
view. On the one hand, they may be extreme and unguarded
expressions of the doctrine of immanence, elaborated in
opposition to Deism and the tyranny of reason, whose mistake
is 'in spaces remote Seeking the Eternal which is always present
to the wise'.[4] On the other hand, they may be expressions of
mystical experience, of the same nature as that to be found in
Angelus Silesius, who asserted that 'I know that without me
God could not exist for a moment. Were I brought to naught
He would yield up the Ghost for lack (of me).' This extra-
ordinary phraseology depicts the mystical drama of love, of the
infinite love between God and man, so great that the loving
subject is unable to live or exist without the loved object and
perishes with it. To express this in metaphysical or theological
terms is an impossibility, it can only be formulated in terms of
experience. However, whether Blake's remarks are taken to
be due to exaggeration or to mystical insight, in neither case is
his essential orthodoxy affected. The truth he was striving to

---

[1] *Jerusalem*, 61. 24–6.   [2] Reynolds, p. 195.
[3] *To Hayley*, 24 May 1804.   [4] *Vala*, 9. 169, 170.

enunciate is that once man has perceived 'the infinite in every-thing', he discovers that he is inseparable from God and that God cannot be separated from him; God apart from man is Blake's idea of abstraction. But this is not pantheism; God indwells the soul 'in such a way that there may exist between the soul and Him a union so close that its analogy is found in the union of subject and object in human knowledge and love, a union which comes of connaturality, which means the possession of the same nature, for indeed by grace we are made precisely "partakers of the divine nature". The soul divinized by grace becomes capable not only of learning about, but of suffering, experiencing, divine things. Without any threat of pantheism, therefore, as Maritain has put it, "the creature receives more than the most daring pantheism could dream of".'[1]

> 'Lo! we are One,' says God to man, 'forgiving all Evil, Not seek-ing recompense.
> Ye are my members.'[2]

To deny the immanence of spirit in man and to regard it as something entirely transcendent is to approach Deism, and to deny any inner relationship between God and man. Over-emphasis upon transcendence leads to dualism, in which God and man are separated by a wide gulf, and no union is possible between them. Consequently, theology must always start, not from God nor from man, but from the God-man, who is beyond and above this antithesis. This important truth, partially neglected by Western thought, but given its true value in Eastern theology, was apprehended by Blake and given expres-sion in his doctrine of the Divine Humanity. 'The Divine Humanity In whose sight all are as dust & who chargeth his Angels with folly.'[3]

Blake, under the influence of Swedenborg, derived this doctrine from two sources. In the first place, he emphasized the humanity of God because He had created mankind. 'Man can have no idea of any thing greater than Man, as a cup cannot contain more than its capaciousness. But God is a man, not because he is so perceiv'd by man, but because he is the creator

---

[1] G. Vann, *Of his Fullness*, 1941, pp. 118, 119.
[2] *Jerusalem*, 4. 20, 21.   Ibid. 49. 30, 31.

of man.'[1] Hence he could declare 'God is Man & exists in us & we in him.'[2] In the second place, Blake maintained that the Incarnation revealed both God's humanity and man's essential nature. Thus he asserted:

> Thou art a Man, God is no more,
> Thy own humanity learn to adore.[3]

And so the redemption wrought by Christ is summed up in these words:

> Nature's Images drawn from Remembrance.
> These are the Sexual Garments, the Abomination of Desolation,
> Hiding the Human Lineaments as with an Ark & Curtains
> Which Jesus rent.[4]

Jesus, by His life and death, thus disclosed the true humanity. 'In Christ the God-Man there is a revelation not only of God but also of His other-self, that is to say, of man; for the Second Hypostasis of the Holy Trinity is Man in the absolute sense, and His revelation means the appearance of a new spiritual and eternal man.'[5] In the Incarnation, man beholds 'A Human Vision! Human Divine, Jesus the Saviour, blessed for ever.'[6] Henceforth 'the eternal face of man abides in the very heart of the Divine Trinity Itself. The Second Hypostasis of Divinity is divine humanity. Christianity overcomes heterogeneity and establishes an absolute kinship between man and God. The transcendent becomes immanent',[5] and Blake beheld

> The Eternal Great Humanity Divine surrounded by
> His Cherubim & Seraphim in ever happy Eternity.[7]

This vision was Blake's from his earliest youth, and received lyric expression in his poem 'The Divine Image', which as it so clearly outlines the doctrine is worth quoting in full.

> To Mercy, Pity, Peace, and Love
> All pray in their distress;
> And to these virtues of delight
> Return their thankfulness.

[1] M.D.L.W., p. 11.
[2] Berkeley, p. 219.
[3] 'Everlasting Gospel', d. 70, 71.
[4] *Milton*, 48. 24–7.
[5] Berdyaev, *Freedom and the Spirit*, op. cit., p. 207.
[6] *Jerusalem*, 40. 46, 47.
[7] *Milton*, 44. 27, 28.

For Mercy, Pity, Peace, and Love
Is God, our father dear,
And Mercy, Pity, Peace and Love
Is Man, his child and care.

For Mercy has a human heart,
Pity a human face,
And Love, the human form divine,
And Peace, the human dress.

Then every man, of every clime,
That prays in his distress,
Prays to the human form divine,
Love, Mercy, Pity, Peace.

And all must love the human form,
In heathen, turk, or jew;
Where Mercy, Love & Pity dwell
There God is dwelling too.

The Kingdom of God, in fact, is that of the God-humanity, in which God is finally in man and man in God.

Blake gave more attention to this doctrine of the divine-humanity than he did to that of the Trinity, although the doctrine of the Trinity equally reconciles the transcendence and immanence of spirit. It is only incidentally that we find any reference to the relationship of the three Persons, and the lack of available material suggests that the belief had no prominent place in Blake's system. Moreover, such information as can be gleaned from isolated passages and remarks is incoherent and at times seems contradictory. Thus we find that on occasion he appears to distinguish between Father, Son, and Holy Ghost, and at other times to identify them to the point of Unitarianism. Apart from his satirical but penetrating comment on Milton's doctrine, written in one of his earliest prophetic books, to the effect that in his thought 'the Father is Destiny, the Son a Ratio of the five senses, & the Holy-ghost Vacuum',[1] the three persons are not mentioned together again until the end of his life, when he penned his version of the Lord's Prayer on the margin of Dr. Thornton's translation, beginning with the invocation: 'Jesus, our Father, who art in heaven call'd by thy Name the Holy Ghost' (p. 3). This last sentence reads like a summary of

---

[1] *Marriage of Heaven and Hell*, p. 6.

Swedenborg, but elsewhere the Persons are differentiated, while each retaining the title of God. Thus Jesus is addressed in language which clearly implies that He is not identical with the Father:

> Lord Saviour, if thou hadst been here our brother had not died,
> And now we know that whatsoever thou wilt ask of God
> He will give it thee; for we are weak women & dare not lift
> Our eyes to the Divine pavilions.[1]

Elsewhere we find: 'Babel mocks, saying there is no God nor Son of God';[2] reference is made to 'the throne of God and the Lamb',[3] to the 'Kingdoms of God & His Christ',[4] and Jesus is called 'the image of the Invisible God',[5] 'the Divine Similitude',[6] and 'the Express image of God'.[7] Similarly, just as the Father is distinguished from the Son, so the Son is distinguished from the Holy Spirit: 'Teach me, O Holy Spirit,' Blake prayed, 'the Testimony of Jesus! let me comprehend wonderous things out of the Divine Law!'[8] His account of his intercourse with Voltaire, reported to Crabb Robinson, equally indicates that the two are not to be identified; Voltaire said to him 'I blasphemed the Son of Man, and it shall be forgiven me. But they (the enemies of Voltaire) blasphemed the Holy Ghost in me, and it shall not be forgiven them.' Two further passages may be adduced in illustration of this distinction. Thus a note on Watson's *Apology* reads: 'Let the Bishop prove that he has not spoken against the Holy Ghost, who in Paine strives with Christendom as in Christ he strove with the Jews' (pp. 4–5); and describing his painting of the Last Judgement, Blake wrote: 'Over the Head of the Saviour & Redeemer The Holy Spirit, like a Dove, is surrounded by a blue Heaven' (p. 85).

Blake also discriminated between the activities of the three Persons; the Father being the Creator,[9] the Son the 'Saviour & Redeemer',[10] and the Holy Ghost the inspirer.[11] But sometimes Blake ascribed the same function to different Persons. Thus he referred to Jesus as the 'Divine Creator & Redeemer',[12] which

[1] *Vala*, 4. 252–5.
[2] *Jerusalem*, 60. 56.
[3] Ibid. 78. 18, 19.
[4] *To Flaxman*, 19 Oct. 1801.
[5] *Milton*, 2. 12.
[6] *Jerusalem*, 38. 11.
[7] *To Butts*, 22 Nov. 1802.
[8] *Jerusalem*, 74. 14, 15.
[9] Job Illus. xv.
[10] *Last Judgment*, p. 85.
[11] *Descriptive Catalogue*, v.
[12] *Jerusalem*, 96. 13.

seems to leave no place for God the Father. Again, he spoke of the Creator becoming incarnate, which seems to dispense with any need of the Son.

Sweet babe, once like thee,
Thy maker lay & wept for me,

Wept for me, for thee, for all,
When he was an infant small.[1]

And Jehovah stood in the Gates of the Victim, & he appeared
A weeping Infant in the Gates of Birth in the midst of Heaven.[2]

In like manner, it is Jehovah Himself that Satan declares will be crucified: 'Thou shalt Thyself be Sacrificed to Me, thy God, on Calvary.'[3] A further confusion of roles is indicated in the statement that 'Jesus is surrounded by Beams of Glory in which are seen all around him Infants emanating from him; these represent the Eternal Births of Intellect from the divine Humanity';[4] this suggests an identity of function between Jesus and the Holy Spirit, Who is an 'Intellectual Fountain'.[5]

From this heterogeneous collection of statements two conclusions emerge. In the first place, Blake spoke of three distinct Persons each of whom is equally God, and at the same time he referred to these three Persons as one. In the second place, Blake differentiated the functions peculiar to each Person, and at the same time allowed the possibility of different Persons performing the same activity. There is only one way in which Blake could have resolved these paradoxes in his own mind, if he ever did, and that was by believing in the doctrine of the Trinity, according to which 'the Father is God, the Son is God: the Holy Ghost is God, And yet there are not three Gods: but one God'. So in the Genesis illustrations, which he began in the last year of his life, Blake depicted the Holy Trinity working together in divine unity.

But always the centre of Blake's religion was Christ, the Divine Humanity, who has revealed the saving love of God in creation and towards mankind. At one time Blake had considered 'that the Creator of this World is a very Cruel Being, & being a Worshipper of Christ, I cannot help saying: "the Son,

---

[1] 'A Cradle Song.'
[2] *Jerusalem*, 63. 16, 17.
[3] *Ghost of Abel*, 42.
[4] *Last Judgment*, p. 85.
[5] *Jerusalem*, 77.

O how unlike the Father!" First God Almighty comes with a Thump on the Head. Then Jesus Christ comes with a balm to heal it.'[1] But as he grew to know Jesus more intimately, Blake perceived that while 'God out of Christ is a consuming fire',[2] in and through the God-man reconciliation is made, the wrath of God being transformed into forgiveness and mercy.

Blake's doctrine of God is remarkable for its flashes of insight and for its lack of detail, both of which derive from his mysticism, for the nearer he approached to God the more vigorously were the barriers between subject and object broken down, and the deeper he was embraced in a relationship so ineffable as to transcend the categories of reason and to render impossible its translation into rational terms. Yet despite his obscurity and his paucity of exposition, Blake had a profound personal knowledge of God, which justified him in proclaiming out of the wealth of his experience: 'O that men would seek immortal moments! O that men would converse with God!'[3]

[1] *Last Judgment*, pp. 92–5.   [2] Reverse of painting in Tate Gallery.
[3] Lavater, 507.

VI

THE FALL AND CREATION

O N the title-page of *Milton*, beneath the naked figure of a man, who, seen from behind, is vanishing in a cloud of swirling vapour, Blake etched the quotation 'To Justify the Ways of God to Men'. The justification of God is the solution of the problem of evil, which inevitably presents itself to the believer in a personal deity whose nature is love. The essence of the problem lies in reconciling the undoubted universality of sin and suffering with the existence of a God who is both good and omnipotent. The perception of the empirical universality of sin has led to a theory of inherited liability to sin, which in turn has compelled the assumption of a primal sin as its source. This primal sin involved a turning away on the part of man from his original condition and destiny, or, in other words, a Fall from his first state.

The expression of the nature of this Fall has undergone a development in the course of time. The first Fall story was based upon the verses at the beginning of the sixth chapter of Genesis, the story of the fallen Angels, and it received elaboration in the Ethiopic Book of Enoch, where the 'Watchers', apostate Angels, descend upon Mount Hermon and there perpetrate the rape. But in the Book of Jubilees, which was written about a hundred years later, at the end of the second century B.C., the Watcher legend was abandoned, and the author turned to the third chapter of Genesis, taking the Adam and Eve myth as his story of the Fall, a choice which had been adumbrated by Ben-Sira. At a later date still, this legend was adopted by St. Paul, and through his influence it became the official Fall story of the Church.

This development indicates that the doctrine of the Fall and Original Sin does not rest upon the historicity of Genesis iii, but 'its true foundations are psychological, based on bed-rock facts of ethical and spiritual experience', accordingly 'the story of Adam and Eve is not and cannot be more than a pictorial façade'.[1] Hence the story or myth by means of which a doctrine

[1] N. P. Williams, *The Ideas of the Fall and Original Sin*, 1927, pp. 31, 215.

is expressed is not an essential part of it, and so Blake's doctrine of the Fall, which next presents itself for consideration, is not to be deemed heterodox solely on the grounds that it does not agree in historical or mythological detail with that of the Church, but only if it disagrees with the doctrine actually taught.

It was characteristic of Blake's restless genius that, although he was much preoccupied with the doctrine of the Fall, he never presented his beliefs with any fullness or consistency, and indeed we find a confusion of four or five myths in his thought. But there was one element of it of which he was quite certain, and about which he never changed his mind, namely, that the Fall did not take place in mundane time; like Origen he believed in a premundane Fall.

The original condition of man in eternity was one of rapturous bliss, to which fallen man, acutely dissatisfied with his present state, looks back with eyes of longing:

> O how unlike those sweet fields of bliss
> Where liberty was justice, & eternal science was mercy.[1]

> O Times remote!
> When Love & Joy were adoration,
> And none impure were deem'd:
> Nor Eyeless Covet,
> Nor Thin-lip'd Envy,
> Nor Bristled Wrath,
> Nor Curled Wantoness.[2]

> Earth was not: nor globes of attraction;
> The will of the Immortal expanded
> Or contracted his all flexible senses;
> Death was not, but eternal life sprung.[3]

But this did not involve any lack of order: 'Many suppose that before the Creation All was Solitude & Chaos. This is the most pernicious Idea that can enter the Mind, as it takes away all sublimity from the Bible & Limits All Existence to Creation & Chaos, To the Time & Space fixed by the Corporeal Vegetative Eye.'[4]

Man was originally androgynous. 'In Eternity Woman is the Emanation of Man; she has No Will of her own. There is no

---

[1] *Vala*, 3. 39, 40.
[3] *Book of Urizen*, 11. 1.
[2] *Book of Los*, 1. 3.
[4] *Last Judgment*, pp. 91–2.

such thing in Eternity as a Female Will.'[1] It seems likely that Blake was indebted to Boehme for the genesis of this idea. 'Adam', wrote the cobbler-mystic, 'was a complete image of God, male and female, and, nevertheless, neither of them separately, but pure like a chaste virgin', and 'Adam was man and wife in one individuality'. Man, therefore, was an integrated whole, with his four elements—thinking or the reason, feeling or the emotions, sensation or the body, and intuition or the spirit—balanced and united. 'All the qualities of the inner and holy body,' said Boehme again in words which exactly represent Blake's thought, 'together with the external ones, were in primordial man attuned in one harmony. Neither of them lived in its own state of desire; but they had their desire in the soul wherein the divine light was manifest. This, the divine light radiated through all the qualities, and produced in them an equal, harmonious temperature.' The disruption of this harmony in 'heaven's darling'[2] led to the Fall.

The account of this disruption is most confusing, owing, in the first instance, to the fact that Blake never completed any one of the several myths he invented to express his ideas. Furthermore, he did not deal directly with the doctrine of the Fall as such, but only used it as a framework around which to build his interpretations of man's psychology. Finally, the obscurity is increased by the fact that his symbolism, which was at first dualistic, later became fourfold, and in recasting some of the earlier passages he failed to eliminate the dualistic basis. However, the myths fall into three definite categories: those in which the Fall is attributed to the attempts of one or other of man's four elements to achieve domination, those in which nature tempts man to desert heaven, and those in which man himself is said to be responsible.[3] To a large extent these

---

[1] Ibid., p. 85.   [2] *Vala*, 2. 24.

[3] One other myth requires notice, viz. that of Satan, according to which in eternity man was the Angel of the Divine Presence, 'elected' for the glory of God. But Satan became envious and began to degrade and vitiate man, who himself was unable to perceive what was happening, because he could not see Satan's activities in outward form—'Truth has bounds, Error none' (*Book of Los*, 2. 5). Hence creation was necessary in order that 'The Man of Sin & Repentance be reveal'd'; 'with bounds to the Infinite putting off the Indefinite' (*Milton*, 30. 4), 'Giving a body to Falshood that it may be cast off for ever' (*Jerusalem*, 12. 13). So creation was an act of mercy and at the same time a fall. This account has no parallel, and differs from the other myths in that no blame is imputed to man.

categories may be considered identical, since in so far as man allowed any one of his warring elements to achieve supremacy, he himself was to blame for his acquiescence, as he was for succumbing to the seduction of nature; nevertheless exposition will be rendered easier if we adhere to this threefold distinction.

Blake asserted that the Fall was due to each one of man's four elements—to reason, to the emotions or passions, to the body, and to the spirit—but these last two are mentioned with less detail or elaboration, whereas the first two receive fuller treatment and are interconnected.

The myths relating to the reason and the passions develop three similar but not identical themes. According to the first, the reason of unfallen man initiated a process of self-contemplation, which led him to perceive himself as an entity separate from eternity. He did not see the purpose of continual transformation, and desired to be 'a solid without fluctuation'.[1] But this self-knowledge also involved man in the perception of his passions, which his reason then sought to dominate. The passions had to find an outlet, but their expression was deemed sinful by his reason, and so the true unity of the soul was split into good and evil, and man was cut off from the ideal.

Albion fell down, a Rocky fragment from Eternity hurl'd
By his own Spectre, who is the Reasoning Power in every Man.[2]

The second theme is not unlike the first. In eternity the One Man lived in peace and inner harmony, the ruling element in his soul being inspired reason. But a conflict arose within him between his reason and his passions, both wanting to be man's sole arbiter.[3] His reason failed and the passions took the lead, but proving unequal to the task, reason again assumed its place, but it was now no longer the inspired intelligence it had been in the beginning but it had become the cold power of logic. Hence the Fall followed upon this estrangement and upon this failure of proper function.

The third theme adds but little to the last. Man's reason attempted to dominate his spirit, but this struggle weakened man and left him vunerable to the assault of the passions, and once again the result was disharmony leading to the Fall.[4]

---

[1] *Book of Urizen*, 11. 4.
[3] *Milton*, 21. 19–21.
[2] *Jerusalem*, 54. 6, 7.
[4] *Vala*, 1. 480–536.

Blake himself provided a convenient summary of these three conceptions when he wrote: 'They were originally one man, who was fourfold; he was self-divided, and his real humanity slain on the stems of generation.'[1]

Blake connected this series of myths with that concerning nature in one passage, where nature is said to have seduced man, and so to have prepared the way for the disintegrating activities of reason and the passions.[2] Nature, in the spiritual and unmaterialized form she possessed in eternity, is called 'the lovely form That drew the body of Man from heaven into this dark Abyss'.[3] Man, 'tempted by the Shadowy female's sweet Delusive cruelty',[4] lost 'heaven & bliss'.[5] But the exact nature of this temptation and the motives which induced man to give way to it are not given, the account being disjointed and incomplete.

In the third category of myths the responsibility for the Fall is quite clearly attributed to man, who is referred to as 'self-exiled from the face of light & shine of morning'.[6] 'Refusing to behold the Divine Image',[7] he 'turn'd his back against the Divine Vision',[8] and consequently fell 'over the Precipice of Eternal Death'.[9] Blake gave two causes for this action, the first of which is somewhat whimsical and finds no echo in any other system. Man, it appears, tired with the energetic labours of eternity, desired a rest and became enamoured of his picture of his own passive self.

Man is a Worm; wearied with joy, he seeks the caves of sleep
Among the Flowers of Beulah, in his selfish cold repose
Forsaking Brotherhood & Universal love, in selfish clay
Folding the pure wings of his mind, seeking the places dark
Abstracted from the roots of Science; then inclos'd around
In walls of Gold we cast him like a Seed into the Earth.[10]

In this 'Sleep, or Chaos, Creation began'.[11]

Underlying this quaint story there is the idea of man becoming self-preoccupied to the vitiation of his loving com-

---

[1] *Descriptive Catalogue*, v.
[2] *Vala*, 7a. 240 ff.
[3] Ibid. 5. 46, 47.
[4] Ibid. 8. 25, 26.
[5] Ibid. 7b. 253.
[6] *Jerusalem*, 19. 13.
[7] *Vala*, 1. 282.
[8] *Jerusalem*, 39. 14.
[9] Ibid. 71. 59.
[10] *Vala*, 9. 625–30.
[11] *Last Judgment*, pp. 80–1.

munion with God, and this leads to the second of Blake's
reasons, to which he made only a passing reference: 'Turning
his Eyes outward to Self, losing the Divine Vision.'[1] It is this
last statement that expresses the element common to all three
categories of myths. It was by rational analysis that man perceived himself to be distinct from God; it was by the allurements
of nature that he concerned himself with that which is outward
instead of perceiving the inner life of brotherhood; it was by
self-will that he turned against the Divine Being. Thus man's
Original Sin, 'The Sin' which 'was begun in Eternity and will
not rest to Eternity Till two Eternitys meet together'[2]—i.e. till
the two eternities of past and future close over the present—
man's Original Sin was the establishing of his own selfhood, the
setting up of himself against God. Blake's position has little
to distinguish it, therefore, from Christian orthodoxy which
teaches that the Original Sin leading to the Fall was one of self-
assertion over against God and the will of God. But whereas,
according to the Catholic faith, that sin was essentially pride,
according to Blake the source of evil was rather the separateness
of the individual soul from the rest of the universe—in other
words, self-consciousness. This conception is paralleled by
much in the thought of Hegel, but by him it is connected with
an unmoral and impersonal Absolute which is irreconcilable
with Biblical theology. By Blake, however, such an impersonal
deity was strongly repudiated, nor was he guilty of the unmoral
monism held by Hegel. Rather, Blake's doctrine is similar to
that theory of 'pre-cosmic vitiation of the whole Life-Force',
presented by the late Dr. Williams.[3] There is indeed nothing
in the doctrine of a pre-mundane Fall necessarily contrary to
the beliefs of Christianity.

It follows that the creation of the world, according to Blake,
took place after the Fall, and, indeed, was a result of the Fall.
But the creation of the world is not to be taken as implying the
creation of man, rather it involved the generation and materialization of man who had been previously created in eternity,

[1] *Vala*, 2. 2.
[2] *Milton*, 14. 10, 11.
[3] Dr. Williams seems to have been guilty of some illogicalities, since he asserted
that the Fall must have taken place at a point in time, and agrees with the
Augustinian position that time and the world were created together, and yet speaks
of a *pre-cosmic* Fall.

although as regards this there is little or no information to be gleaned from Blake's works. All his myths assume the existence of man in eternity, and little is said of how he came to be there. Because of this silence, it has been held that Blake did accept monism. But, as we have seen, Blake did maintain a distinction between the Creator and the creature, and scattered references suggest that this must not be applied solely to fallen man, but also to Eternal Man; thus, for example, he spoke of 'A ruin'd Man, a ruin'd building of God'.[1] This was said of man in time, yet it obviously implies that whereas fallen man is ruined, he never ceases to be a building of God, i.e. the saying must not be interpreted to mean that God built a ruin, but that a creation of God has been ruined, ruined, it may be added, by the Fall. However, the most direct answer to the charge of monism is given by the very doctrine of the Fall itself; it was man who fell, not God, and man fell, according to Blake, by emphasizing his own selfhood, and by perceiving his distinction from the Divine Being.

The first result of the Fall then was that Man's 'eternal life like a dream was obliterated',[2] and he trembled on 'the verge of Non Existence',[3] 'ready to fall into Non-Entity'.[4] 'In pride of Selfhood unwieldy stretching out into Non Entity',[5] he was about to be precipitated into 'the Void Outside of Existence',[6] for 'Mighty was the draught of Voidness to draw Existence in'.[7] It was to prevent this that the world was created and 'Limit was put to Eternal Death':[8]

> whatever is visible to the Generated Man
> Is a Creation of mercy & love from the Satanic Void.[9]

'If the matter of this world were broken,' said Boehme, 'as it will be broken one day in the future, the soul would have stood in eternal death, in the darkness.' To save man from this calamity the Lord caused a deep sleep to fall upon him, 'he fell asleep to the angelic world, and awoke relatively to the external world'. 'After the lust of the spirit of this world had

---

[1] *Milton*, 43. 16.   [2] *Book of Urizen*, v. 3.
[3] *Vala*, 2. 21.
[4] *Jerusalem*, 43. 15.
[5] Ibid. 43. 53.   [6] *Milton*, 48. 37.
[7] *Vala*, 2. 18.   [8] Ibid. 4. 274, 275.
[9] *Jerusalem*, 13. 44–5.

conquered in Adam, he fell asleep. Then his celestial body became flesh and blood, and his strong power became rigid bones.' So Blake believed that in his 'Chaotic State of Sleep . . . the whole World was Created',[1]

> so permitted because
> It was the best possible in the State called Satan to save
> From Death Eternal & to put off Satan Eternally.[2]
>
> For the Divine Lamb, Even Jesus who is the Divine Vision,
> Permitted all, lest Man should fall into Eternal Death.[3]

Blake, therefore, considered that the creation, in the first instance, 'was an act of Mercy'.[4] Man 'was made receptive of Generation thro' mercy'.[5]

> We behold it is of Divine
> Mercy alone, of Free Gift and Election that we live:
> Our virtues & Cruel Goodness have deserv'd Eternal Death;[6]

yet God built 'a Bower for heaven's darling in the grizly deep',[7] and created 'a World of Generation from the World of Death'.[8] But the effect of this was to petrify 'all the Human Imagination into rock & sand',[9] the 'Mortal Body being render'd a Permanent Statue'.[10] The five senses overwhelmed man and confined his vision, shutting out heaven, submerging him in time and space and leaving nothing 'except this finite wall of flesh'.[11]

> Their eyes, their ears, nostrils & tongues roll outwards, they
> behold
> What is within now seen without.[12]

A process of externalization was taking place, whereby the universe, which once with man was a conscious element of the Divine Unity, is perceived by man as independent and multiple; with the Fall an antithesis has arisen between the One and the Many. 'Separation from God and from the original sources of spiritual life, the disunion and division of being produced by an

[1] *Jerusalem*, 27.   [2] *Vala*, 8. 281–3.
[3] Ibid. 2. 262–3.   [4] *Last Judgment*, pp. 91–2.
[5] *Jerusalem*, 53. 27.   [6] *Milton*, 14. 32–4.
[7] *Vala*, 2. 24.   [8] *Jerusalem*, 58. 18.
[9] *Vala*, 2. 38.   [10] *Last Judgment*, p. 79.
[11] *Europe*, 80–93.   [12] *Vala*, 2. 54, 55.

irrational orientation of it, are reflected in the psychical and material world.'[1] It was with this thought in mind that Blake referred to the tradition 'that Man anciently contain'd in his mighty limbs all things in Heaven & Earth';[2] but now 'The Starry Heavens all were fled from the mighty limbs of Albion'.[3] The meaning of these ambiguous statements is brought out in the works of Nicolas Berdyaev, who, deeply influenced by Boehme, is one of the most prominent thinkers of the present epoch, and from him we take the following extended quotations, which illuminate so clearly Blake's otherwise obscure idea.

'Man is separated from God and the world from man, so that the world becomes something external to man which forces him to submit to its own laws. Man loses his spiritual independence. He begins to be determined from without and not from within. The sun ceases to shine upon him and to be the light of the world as before. It now becomes part of the nature which is external to man, the life of which depends entirely on illumination from without. The whole universe being separated from God ceases to have an inner radiance; it needs a source of light exterior to itself. The principal result of the Fall is just this loss of inner illumination and the subordination of everything to an external source. When man dwells in God then the cosmos is in man; he has the sun within himself. When God and man are separated the cosmos and man are separated too.'[4]

Blake believed that 'in the spiritual man is included the cosmos and all creation. But the cosmos was violently separated from fallen man so that it became something external to him to which he is enslaved.'[5] Nevertheless, 'in the interior, spiritual, world . . . the cosmos is presented to us in all the beauty of its inner life'.[6]

> In your own Bosom you bear your Heaven
> And Earth & all you behold; tho' it appears Without, it is Within.[7]

And so Blake, looking at nature with the eyes of vision, believed

> Each grain of Sand,
> Every Stone on the Land,
> Each rock & each hill,
> Each fountain & rill,

[1] Berdyaev, op. cit., p. 124.   [2] Jerusalem, 27.
[3] Ibid. 70. 33.   [4] Berdyaev, op. cit., p. 201.
[5] Berdyaev, op. cit., p. 198.   [6] Ibid., p. 41.
[7] Jerusalem, 71. 17, 18.

Each herb & each tree,
Mountain, hill, earth & sea,
Cloud, Meteor & Star,
Are Men seen Afar.[1]

as the Seed waits Eagerly watching for its flower & fruit . . .
So Man looks out in tree & herb & fish & bird & beast
Collecting up the scatter'd portions of his immortal body
Into the Elemental forms of every thing that grows. . . .
. . . wherever a grass grows
Or a leaf buds, The Eternal Man is seen, is heard, is felt,
And all his sorrows, till he reassumes his ancient bliss.[2]

The cosmos then is an externalization of man's inner life due to
the Fall, and all mankind is descended from the one man:

From Albion's Loins fled all Peoples and Nations of the Earth,
Fled with the noise of Slaughter, & the stars of heaven fled.[3]

To the same effect, Boehme declared, 'The sum of all mankind
constitutes the one original Adam.'

Blake therefore considered that the Fall resulted in the
externalization of man's inner nature and the creation of the
natural man. At this point Blake provided a clear indication
of the further course of events, in the chapter-headings he
transcribed in the illuminated autograph of Genesis which he
began for John Linnell in 1826 or 1827:

Chap. I. The Creation of the Natural Man.

Chap. II. The Natural Man divided into Male & Female, & of
the Tree of Life, & of the Tree of Good and Evil.

Chap. III. Of Sexual Nature, & of its Fall into Generation and
Death.

Chap. IV. How Generation and Death took Possession of the
Natural Man & Of the Forgiveness of Sins written on the
Murderer's Forehead.

From this outline it is evident that the next step in man's dis-
integration was the division into sexes.

Man, as we have seen, was originally androgynous—
'Humanity is far above Sexual organisation'—and to that condition he will eventually return when regenerated. 'Sexes must

---

[1] *To Butts*, 2 Oct. 1800, 25–32.   [2] *Vala*, 8. 554, 557–9, 577–9.
[3] *Vala*, 2. 43, 44.

vanish & cease to be when Albion arises from his dread repose.'[1]
The division into male and female, and the sexual intercourse
attendant thereon, is an abhorrence to heaven,

> Eternity shudder'd when they saw
> Man begetting his likeness
> On his own divided image.[2]

This severance is part of the externalization of the inner life of
man, who individualized his sexual passion, and it separated
from him 'a female bright':

> one dread morn of goary blood
> The manhood was divided, for the gentle passions, making way
> Thro' the infinite labyrinths of the heart & thro' the nostrils
> issuing
> In odorous stupefaction, stood before the Eyes of Man
> A female bright.[3]

A parallel idea is to be found in Boehme: 'Adam having lost the
power to recognise the true woman, the eternal virgin within
himself, it was necessary that he should have an external
objective substitute to whom he might be attracted, so as to
stimulate his power to love; which would have entirely died out
without such an object.' But this view is of Greek and pagan
origin and cannot be reconciled with the Bible, which speci-
fically states 'male and female created he them'. However,
there is an important element of truth underlying this belief.
Human sexuality points to a vast cleavage in human nature
which comes out in this sphere with especial force. Connected
with all sexual love there are two ineradicable features: a sense
of shame and a longing which cannot be satisfied, both of which
derive from the Fall. The shame arises from the entrance of sin
into the sex relationship so that sex and spirit are divided; the
longing comes from the division in the union, due also to sin,
and the corresponding incapacity to give satisfaction. Hence
Blake declared:

> The Sexes sprung from Shame & Pride,
> Blow'd in the morn; in evening died;
> But Mercy chang'd Death into Sleep;
> The Sexes rose to work & weep.[4]

---

[1] *Jerusalem*, 92. 13–14.
[2] *Book of Urizen*, vi. 2.
[3] *Vala*, 7a. 279–82.
[4] 'To Tirzah', stanza 2.

The next feature in Blake's transcription of Genesis that calls for consideration is the connexion of the Trees of Knowledge and Life with the Fall. The eating of the apple, which in the Bible is the first and only cause of the Fall, was to Blake the climax of error. He interpreted the eating of the Tree of Knowledge as issuing in 'The Combats of Good & Evil', and the eating of the Tree of Life as producing 'The Combats of Truth & Error'.[1] According to Blake, the division of the universe into the black and white of good and evil is a false system, preventing a true valuation of it, for it is essentially holy; morality and the moral law are signs of the Fall, for in heaven 'they are no longer talking of what is Good & Evil, or of what is Right or Wrong, & puzzling themselves in Satan's Labyrinth, But are Conversing with Eternal Realities'.[2] It is possible to interpret the knowledge of good and evil as the Fall. The capacity to know good and evil involves the loss of innocence, and, therefore, an estrangement from God; thus knowledge is the loss of Paradise and sin is the attempt to know good and evil. Moral consciousness presupposes the dualism of good and evil, and, therefore, had its source in the Fall. But here again Blake was far from explicit, and we are left wondering how he himself would have developed those disconnected flashes of insight, of which this is an example, and with which his work abounds.

In tracing Blake's ideas of the Fall and Creation we have seen that he considered the latter an act of mercy which saved man from plunging headlong into the abyss of non-existence; but he also elaborated another cause for the creation, which is, however, complementary and not contradictory to the first, viz. that it might be a means of regaining the Divine Unity. 'O holy Generation, Image of regeneration.'[3]

> This World is all a Cradle for the erred wandering Phantom,
> Rock'd by Year, Month, Day & Hour.[4]

It is

> the beautiful Mundane Shell,
> The Habitation of the Spectres of the Dead, & the Place
> Of Redemption & of awaking again into Eternity.[5]

---

[1] *Last Judgment*, pp. 86, 90.   [2] Ibid., pp. 90–1.
[3] *Jerusalem*, 7. 65.   [4] Ibid. 56. 8, 9.
[5] Ibid. 59. 7–9.

So certain was Blake of this, that he went to the extreme of contending:

> Nor can any consummate bliss without being Generated
> On Earth.[1]

The teleological function of mundane life was constantly expressed in his later works.

> all this Vegetable World appear'd on my left Foot
> As a bright sandal form'd immortal of precious stones & gold.
> I stooped down & bound it on to walk forward thro'
> Eternity.[2]

In view of this there can be little doubt that in Blake's mind the Creator was no demiurge. 'The Bible says that God formed Nature perfect, but that Man perverted the order of Nature, since which time the Elements are fill'd with the Prince of Evil, who has the power of the air.'[3] 'Let it be remember'd that creation is God descending according to the weakness of man.'[4] In the final consummation, Nature herself will be redeemed, for this world was destined to be the 'Birthplace of the Lamb of God incomprehensible'.[5] This would appear to establish beyond doubt the identity of the Creator and the supreme God Himself, but this assertion must be questioned in view of Blake's references to the 'elohim'. 'Nature', he said, 'is a Vision of the Science of the Elohim.'[6] Elsewhere he wrote, 'the whole World was Created by the Elohim';[7] and when Crabb Robinson reports: 'I referred to the commencement of Genesis—In the beginning God created the Heavens and the Earth. But I gained nothing by this, for I was triumphantly told that this God was not Jehovah but the Elohim', we seem thrown back once more on the doctrine of a demiurge. But recourse to Boehme's teaching, which is such an invaluable aid to the understanding of Blake, reveals the true nature of these beings. 'Creation could, however, become actually complete only by means of the activity of all the seven divine spirits. It is therefore true that in one sense it was not God, the primordial Cause, that directly created the world, but the *elohims* or

[1] Ibid. 86. 42, 43.
[2] *Milton*, 23. 12–14.
[3] Watson, p. 6.
[4] Lavater, 630.
[5] *Jerusalem*, 7. 67.
[6] *Milton*, 31. 65.
[7] *Jerusalem*, 27.

"powers" that created it by means of the power received from the fundamental causation.' These seven Spirits are really 'only one spirit', and are revelations of the Trinity on the different planes of existence, distinguished by Boehme. Thus the 'elohims' of Boehme find their place in Blake's system, and in the aggregate he called them the Angel of the Divine Presence, and sometimes Jehovah Elohim.[1] They are also referred to as the Seven Eyes of God,[2] and as in Boehme are really one spirit, for 'The Seven are one within the other'.[3] This is entirely consistent, therefore, with Blake's view of the Creation as an act of divine mercy and as a means of regeneration. 'The line of the almighty' has been 'drawn out upon' the chaos produced by the Fall, so that 'man or beast can exist'.[4]

Although creation is a manifestation of divine love, the situation produced by the Fall is far from being a happy one. 'The fall produced only generation and death', Blake told Crabb Robinson. The 'Corporeal & Mortal Body—that originated with the Fall & was call'd Death & cannot be removed but by a Last Judgment'.[5]

> No more could they rise at will
> In the infinite void, but bound down
> To earth by their narrowing perceptions
> They lived a period of years;
> Then left a noisom body
> To the jaws of devouring darkness.[6]

'Satan now awakes Sin & death & Hell to celebrate with him the birth of war & misery; while the Lion seizes the bull; the tyger, the horse: the vulture & the eagle contend over the lamb.'[7] Man's existence is no longer one of eternal brotherhood, but one of hatred, strife, and death. Man is 'separate from Man';[8] under the power of Satan 'the Whole Creation Groans to be deliver'd'.[9] 'Reality was Forgot, & the Vanities of Time & Space only Remember'd & call'd Reality.'[10] 'The Bible tells

---

[1] *Last Judgment*, pp. 80–1.
[2] *Vala*, 8. 405–13.
[3] Ibid. 1. 547.
[4] *Descriptive Catalogue*, xv.
[5] *Last Judgment*, pp. 92–5.
[6] *Book of Urizen*, ix. 4.
[7] Reverse of painting.
[8] *Jerusalem*, 28. 12.
[9] *Last Judgment*, pp. 92–5.
[10] Ibid., pp. 71–2.

me that the plan of Providence was Subverted at the Fall of Adam & that it was not restored till Christ',[1] who comes that He

> may find a way for my banished ones to return.
> Fear not, O little Flock, I come. Albion shall rise again.[2]

[1] Watson, p. 9.   [2] *Jerusalem*, 29. 25, 26.

VII

HIS DOCTRINE OF CHRIST AND OF REDEMPTION

THE Person of Christ has powerfully fascinated many of the world's great literary figures, among whom may be mentioned Dostoievsky, Tolstoi, D. H. Lawrence, and by no means least William Blake. Blake, indeed, who called himself 'a Soldier of Christ',[1] could scarcely write a letter, even on matters entirely commercial, without some reference to the spiritual world and to 'our Lord & Saviour'. But like so many other individualists, who have lacked the sane equilibrium of the Catholic tradition, he conceived Christ in his own likeness, seizing on those features of His complex and vivid personality which most appealed to his genius, and neglecting those to which by nature he was incapable of responding. Thus in Blake's hands Christ became a rebel hero, whose facial characteristics even were those of Blake himself:

> The Vision of Christ that thou dost see
> Is my Vision's Greatest Enemy:
> Thine has a great hook nose like thine,
> Mine has a snub nose like to mine.[2]

Nor is this to be explained away as poetic imagery: the same thought is recorded in prose amongst a number of fragmentary jottings. 'I always thought that Jesus Christ was a Snubby or I should not have worship'd him, if I had thought he had been one of those long spindle nosed rascals.' Despite such exaggerations, to which Blake was always prone, his portrait of Jesus is at once both fresh and stimulating, while his Christology, which remains only in bold outlines, is in the main a rephrasing of orthodox doctrine in the terms of his own idiom.

The term 'Incarnation' was never employed by Blake, probably because he considered it was apt to be confusing, in so far as it tended to encourage the view of nature accepted by the man of single vision. Nevertheless, the substance of his belief is identical with that of the Church. To Christ Blake applied the words from the prologue of St. John 'and dwelt

---

[1] *To Butts,* 10 Jan. 1802.   [2] 'Everlasting Gospel', a. 1–4.

among us', and said, 'God becomes as we are, that we may be
as he is',[1] which might almost be a free translation of St.
Athanasius' dictum: 'he, indeed, assumed humanity that we
might become God.' 'Did not Jesus descend and become a
servant?'[2] asked Blake, and gave his own answer elsewhere in
verse:

> Sweet babe, once like thee,
> Thy maker lay and wept for me,
>
> Wept for me, for thee, for all,
> When he was an infant small.[3]
>
> He becomes an infant small;
> He becomes a man of woe.[4]
>
> He became a little child.[5]

Implicit in Blake's words is the doctrine of the two natures,
Jesus was both God and man, 'for the source of life Descends
to be a weeping babe',[6] and 'he appeared A weeping Infant in
the Gates of Birth'.[7] Hence Blake believed in our Lord who 'is
the word of God',[8] and proclaimed

> Faith in God the dear Saviour who took on the likeness of men,
> Becoming obedient to death, even the death of the Cross.[9]

It was Jesus, the 'image of the Invisible God',[10] who 'took on
Sin in the Virgin's Womb'.[11]

This reference to the 'Virgin's womb' should not be taken to
imply that Blake accepted the doctrine of the Virgin Birth. On
the contrary, his coupling of the Virgin Mary and Johanna
Southcott, in the title of a random quatrain, indicates that he
rejected the traditional belief, for Johanna, a Methodist servant
girl, claimed to be the woman of the Apocalypse and, at the age
of sixty-four, announced herself pregnant of the holy child
'Shiloh' by the agency of the Holy Ghost: a claim refuted by her
death and subsequent autopsy which revealed that her preg-
nancy was nothing more than dropsy. In one passage Blake
gave his reinterpretation of the events that preceded the Nativity,

---

[1] *No Natural Religion*, 11.
[2] Bacon.
[3] 'A Cradle Song.'
[4] 'On Another's Sorrow.'
[5] 'The Lamb.'
[6] *Vala*, 2. 369, 370.
[7] *Jerusalem*, 63. 16, 17.
[8] Lavater, 630.
[9] *Milton*, 24. 57, 58.
[10] Ibid. 2. 12.
[11] 'Everlasting Gospel', b. 55.

using them in order to emphasize his doctrine of unconditional forgiveness. Mary is declared to have been immoral,

> Was Jesus Born of a Virgin Pure
> With narrow Soul & looks demure?
> If he intended to take on Sin
> The Mother should an Harlot been,
> Just such a one as Magdalen
> With seven devils in her Pen;
> Or were Jew Virgins still more Curst,
> And more sucking devils nurst?[1]

Joseph taxes her with infidelity, and is answered: 'Art thou more pure Than thy Maker who forgiveth Sins & calls again Her that is Lost?'[2] So moving is Mary's reply that Joseph forgives her, saying that an angel had appeared to him in a dream and had announced, 'Fear not then to take To thee Mary thy Wife, for she is with Child by the Holy Ghost.'[3] But in view of what has gone before this cannot be interpreted as an orthodox affirmation, rather it means that the conception of Jesus was due to the Holy Ghost simply because Mary, 'ignorant of crime in the midst of a corrupted Age',[4] yielded to the impulse of true desire which is a command from God. The essential features of this account that requires to be noted is, not that Mary was immoral, but that the idea of a parthenogenesis is rejected and Jesus' conception attributed to the union of two human beings. This theory, novel to a certain extent in Blake's day, is accepted by some modern believers on the grounds that the Virgin Birth is a difficulty rather than a help in Christology, since when the Son of God took upon Him our manhood, His birth should have been completely natural in all its circumstances. There is, therefore, more to be said for Blake's theory than is at first apparent, and in our ultimate assessment of his theology care must be taken not to deny him the title of Christian because of his repudiation of the Virgin Birth, if there seem other good reasons to classify him as such.

Whatever the circumstances of Jesus' birth, Blake was quite convinced that He was God and man, the Divine Humanity, 'to whom the Ancients look'd and saw his day afar off, with trembling & amazement',[5] 'waiting with patience for the fulfil-

---

[1] 'Everlasting Gospel', i. 1–8.   [2] *Jerusalem*, 61. 6, 7.
[3] Ibid. 61. 26, 27.   [4] *Last Judgment*, pp. 80–1.   [5] *Jerusalem*, 3.

ment of the Promise Divine'.[1] So, in the fullness of time, 'the Lamb of God, the Saviour became apparent on Earth as the Prophets had foretold'.[2] His Incarnation was the climax of creation, and His crucifixion was implicit in the Fall, and in a sense was coincidental with the Fall, for Adam and Eve were the first murderers of the Christ, since they killed the divine life in their souls.

In outlining his conception of the Incarnate Lord Blake was entirely consistent; the character-study of Christ which he wrote in his early manhood he exactly reproduced in his old age. To Blake Jesus was and remained always a rebel; One who had come to free mankind from the shackles of the law, and who carried out His mission with the utmost thoroughness.

'Hear how he has given his sanction to the law of ten commandments: did he not mock at the sabbath and so mock the sabbath's God? murder those who were murder'd because of him? turn away the law from the woman taken in adultery? steal the labor of others to support him? bear false witness when he omitted making a defence before Pilate? covet when he pray'd for his disciples, and when he bid them shake off the dust of their feet against such as refused to lodge them? I tell you, no virtue can exist without breaking these ten commandments. Jesus was all virtue, and acted from impulse, not from rules.'[3]

Twenty-five years later Blake repeated this identical theme in his 'Everlasting Gospel':

> He mock'd the Sabbath, & he mock'd
> The Sabbath's God, & he unlocked

[1] *Vala*, 7b. 292. Blake made two statements which seem to suggest Adoptionism, viz. 'Know that after Christ's death, he became Jehovah' (*Marriage of Heaven and Hell*, p. 6), and 'On my enquiring how he reconciled this with the sanctity and divine qualities of Jesus, he said He was not then become the Father'. If their surface meaning be correct, Jesus according to Blake was not God and man but merely a man of outstanding qualities who achieved divinity. But this cannot be reconciled with what Blake said elsewhere, particularly his repeated assertion of the need for Jesus to descend and save. Accordingly, the first statement must mean that after His death Christ was worshipped as the God of morality (Jehovah being used in this instance, as in others, in a derogatory sense, referring to the non-existent God of this world, or Satan, who is 'Worship'd by the Names Divine of Jesus & Jehovah', 'Gates of Paradise'), and the second statement was another example of Blake setting out to confuse, a tendency which we have seen reason to suspect underlay many of his sayings to Crabb Robinson.

[2] *Jerusalem*, 27.   [3] *Marriage of Heaven and Hell*, p. 23.

> The Evil spirits from their Shrines,
> And turn'd Fishermen to Divines;
> O'erturn'd the Tent of Secret Sins,
> & its Golden cords & Pins—
> 'Tis the Bloody Shrine of War
> Pinn'd around from Star to Star,
> Halls of justice, hating Vice,
> Where the devil Combs his lice.
> He turn'd the devils into Swine
> That he might tempt the Jews to dine;
> Since which, a Pig has got a look
> That for a Jew may be mistook.
> 'Obey your parents.'—What says he?
> 'Woman, what have I to do with thee?
> 'No Earthly Parents I confess:
> 'I am doing my Father's Business.'
> He scorn'd Earth's Parents, scorn'd Earth's God,
> And mock'd the one & the other's Rod;
> His Seventy Disciples sent
> Against Religion & Government:
> They by the Sword of Justice fell
> And him their Cruel Murderer tell.
> He left his Father's trade to roam
> A wand'ring Vagrant without Home;
> And thus he others' labour stole
> That he might live above Controll.
> The Publicans & Harlots he
> Selected for his Company,
> And from the Adultress turn'd away
> God's righteous Law, that lost its Prey. (i. 17–48.)

The perverseness of this account is at once apparent; few men have so ruthlessly twisted the Gospel records to support their own theories, and yet even here there is a substratum of truth, for Jesus did come to liberate men from the burden of the law, 'For Christ is the end of the law unto righteousness to every one that believeth',[1] 'Having abolished in his flesh the enmity, even the law of commandments contained in ordinances.'[2] To the contemporaries of His Incarnate Life, especially the Pharisees, Jesus was indeed a law-breaker, and it is to be noted that the passage quoted above from the 'Everlasting Gospel' is

---

[1] *Romans* x. 14.
[2] *Ephesians* ii. 15.

put in the mouth of Caiaphas, but it is also a complete expression of Blake's own ideas, hence his affirmation

> Jesus died because he strove
> Against the current of this Wheel; its Name
> Is Caiaphas, the dark preacher of Death,
> Of sin, of sorrow, & of punishment:
> Opposing Nature! It is Natural Religion;
> But Jesus is the bright Preacher of Life
> Creating Nature from this fiery Law,
> By self-denial & forgiveness of Sin.[1]

It is unfortunate that Blake chose to express this idea, which is the basis of his ethics, in such an extreme form, which, although arresting and provoking, is manifestly an over-literalistic misinterpretation of the Evangelists' records.

However much Blake was prepared to recreate Jesus in his own likeness, there were certain of His actions that he could not explain away, and consequently he maintained that He was subject to error. ' "Christ," said he, "took much after his mother (the law), and in that respect was one of the worst of men." On my enquiring an explanation, he said, "There was his turning the money changers out of the Temple. He had no right to do that." ' Again, he considered that 'He should not have attacked the Government. He had no business with such matters.' With the failure of the French Revolution, Blake had become disillusioned and cynical about political action; pacifistic in outlook, he concentrated more and more upon the inner life of the spirit; hence in so far as Jesus did not conform to the same attitude, He was wrong! Blake, however, misunderstood the account in the Gospels; Jesus never attacked the Government, for to do so would have been to place Himself at the head of a national Messianic movement, which was contrary to His mission.

Nevertheless, whatever faults Blake imagined he saw in Jesus, they were insignificant compared with those features of His character for which he had a whole-hearted admiration. 'The greatest of all characters,' wrote Lavater (16), 'no doubt, was he, who, free from all trifling accidental helps, could see objects through one grand immutable medium, always at hand, and

---

[1] *Jerusalem*, 77.

proof against illusion and time, reflected by every object, and invariably traced through all the fluctuations of things.' 'This was Christ', Blake commented. 'Beauty', reads another aphorism (383), 'we call the MOST VARIED ONE, the MOST UNITED VARIETY. Could there be a man who should harmoniously unite each variety of knowledge and of powers— were he not the most beautiful? were he not your god?' Which passage Blake summarized in the words 'This is our Lord', underlining, at the same time, the final word 'god'.

In the Incarnation, Christ, 'the Good Shepherd',[1] adopted a means whereby the Divine might be revealed to weak mankind, in a manner at once intelligible without being overpowering. The purpose of His descent to earth was summed up for Blake in the Crucifixion, and in his painting *Christ in the Lap of Truth* the Holy Child has His arms outstretched in cruciform fashion, indicating that the Cross reveals Christ's relationship to truth. In attempting to define this relationship, Blake's ideas were as varied as they were multiple. Christ came to create States, to bring liberty, to teach forgiveness. His death on the Cross wrought the destruction of the Selfhood, the deliverance from the power of Satan whose system was thereby made apparent, the rending of the veil of flesh and the revelation of the spiritual body; it was an example of martyrdom and supreme self-sacrifice, being an enacted exhortation to brotherhood, and the opening of the way back to Eternity. Each one of these conceptions provides an excellent starting-point for a theory of the Atonement, yet not one of them was worked out fully by Blake, and little notice was taken by him of their implications. According to Crabb Robinson, Blake 'spoke of the Atonement. Said, "It is a horrible doctrine. If another man pay your debt, I do not forgive it" '; but in another passage relating the same incident important qualifying words were introduced, and it appears that Blake was referring to the Atonement 'in the ordinary Calvinistic sense'. Thus Blake repudiated any penal or juridical theory of the Atonement:

> Must the Wise die for an Atonement? does Mercy endure Atonement?
> No! It is Moral Severity & destroys Mercy in its Victim.[2]

---

[1] *Vala*, 1. 194.
[2] *Jerusalem*, 39. 25, 26.

Doth Jehovah Forgive a Debt only on condition that it shall
Be Payed?[1]

O God, thou art Not an Avenger![2]

But the essence of the doctrine of the Atonement is that God in
Christ reconciles mankind to Himself, and the inauguration of
this 'New covenant' between God and man, this at-one-ment,
took place when Jesus died on the Cross. The various theories
of the Atonement have been attempts to define how this great
change in man's relation to God, of which Christian faith and
life are the evidence, has been effected; but the Church as a
whole has never accepted any particular explanation, proclaiming with Blake, as a fact of experience, 'The Death of
Jesus set me free,'[3] while advancing no theory of how this has
taken place. This being so, it will be seen that Blake's rejection
of the penal theory did not involve his condemnation of the
doctrine of the Atonement in its entirety, and indeed the ideas
already listed show, beyond all doubt, that he did accept the
doctrine in its essentials and was eager to advance his own
interpretations of it.

At the Incarnation, Christ assumed the 'dark Satanic Body',[4]
'the Maternal Humanity',[5] 'the Sexual Garments, the Abomi-
nation of Desolation',[6] which hide 'the Human Lineaments as
with an Ark & Curtains'.[7]

> by his Maternal Birth he is that Evil-One
> And his Maternal Humanity must be put off Eternally,
> Lest the Sexual Generation swallow up Regeneration.
> Come Lord Jesus, take on thee the Satanic Body of Holiness.[8]

So the Saviour, the 'Universal Humanity—who is One Man,
blessed for Ever'—received 'the Integuments woven';[9] He took
to Himself 'the dark Satanic body in the Virgin's womb'.[10]
Then

> was the Lamb of God condemn'd to Death.
> They nail'd him upon the tree of Mystery, weeping over him
> And then mocking & then worshipping, calling him Lord & King.[11]

[1] Ibid. 61. 17, 18.   [2] Ibid. 46. 28.
[3] 'To Tirzah.'   [4] Vala, 8. 194.
[5] Jerusalem, 90. 36.   [6] Milton, 48. 25.
[7] Ibid. 48. 26.   [8] Jerusalem, 90. 35-8.
[9] Vala, 8. 230, 231.   [10] Ibid. 239.
[11] Ibid. 321-3.

At the Crucifixion 'the Body of Death'[1] was stripped 'from off the lamb of God' and 'his glory' was manifested.[2]

> He puts off the clothing of blood, he redeems the spectres from their bonds.[3]

On the Cross 'death Eternal is put off Eternally',[4] and Christ rends the veil of flesh which obscures the spirit—'A Veil the Saviour born & dying rends'.[5] He gave

> his vegetated body
> To be cut off & separated, that the Spiritual body may be Reveal'd[6]

> He died as a Reprobate, he was Punish'd as a Transgressor.
> Glory! Glory! Glory! to the Holy Lamb of God.[7]

Hence Blake's hymn of praise:

> Glory, Glory, Glory to the holy Lamb of God
> Who now beginneth to put off the dark Satanic body.
> Now we behold redemption. Now we know that life Eternal
> Depends alone upon the Universal hand, & not in us
> Is aught but death.[8]

Underlying this conception of the Atonement consisting in the revelation of the true nature of reality is the equally important idea that the Crucifixion frees man from the law, for 'the Infernal Veil'[9] is both the outward crust of matter, the mortal body, hiding the spirit within, and also 'the whole Druid Law',[10]

> which Jesus rends & . . . removes away
> From the Inner Sanctuary, a False Holiness hid within the Centre.[11]

So 'the Lamb of God has rent the Veil of Mystery',[12] thereby

> Saving those who have sinned from the punishment of the Law
> (In pity of the punisher whose state is eternal death)
> And keeping them from Sin by the mild counsels of his love.[13]

[1] *Milton*, 14. 25.   [2] *Vala*, Add. Frag.
[3] Ibid. 8. 234.   [4] Ibid. 238.
[5] *Jerusalem*, 55. 16.   [6] *Vala*, 8. 263, 264.
[7] *Milton*, 14. 27, 28.   [8] *Vala*, 8. 193–7.
[9] *Jerusalem*, 69. 38.   [10] Ibid. 39.
[11] Ibid. 39. 40.   [12] *Vala*, 8. 552.
[13] *Jerusalem*, 35. 6–8.

Thus

the Divine Mercy
Steps beyond and Redeems Man in the Body of Jesus;[1]

so that

the Perfect
May live in glory, redeem'd by Sacrifice of the Lamb.[2]

The revelation of the spirit, and this overthrowing of the power of the law, involve also the unmasking of Satan, for 'you cannot behold him till he be reveal'd in his System',[3] and this is accomplished by the Crucifixion which reveals 'to all in heaven And all on Earth, the Temple & the Synagogue of Satan, & Mystery'.[4] So 'Christ comes . . . to deliver those who were bound under the Knave'.[5] The fallacy of the Satanic system of law and morality is once and for all demonstrated by the Cross, for it was because of his opposition to those same beliefs that Jesus was crucified.

Jesus, the image of the Invisible God,
Became its prey, a curse, an offering and an atonement
For Death Eternal.[6]

'Why did Christ come? Was it not to abolish the Jewish Imposture? Was not Christ marter'd because he taught that God loved all Men & was their father & forbad all contention for Worldly prosperity?'[7] 'What Jesus came to remove was the Heathen or Platonic Philosophy, which blinds the Eye of Imagination, The Real Man.'[8] 'He who does Forgive Sin is Crucified as an Abettor of Criminals, & he who performs Works of Mercy in Any Shape whatever is punish'd &, if possible, destroy'd, not thro' envy or Hatred or Malice but thro' Self Righteousness that thinks it does God service, which God is Satan.'[9] Because of His attitude to the law, Satan and his minions leagued together

To judge the Lamb of God to Death as a murderer & robber:
As it is written, he was number'd among the transgressors.[10]

---

[1] Ibid. 36. 53, 54.
[2] Ibid. 18. 26, 27.
[3] Ibid. 29. 10.
[4] *Vala*, 8. 339, 340.
[5] *Last Judgment*, pp. 86, 90.
[6] *Milton*, 2. 12–14.
[7] Watson, pp. 4–5.
[8] Berkeley, p. 241.
[9] *Last Judgment*, pp. 92–5.
[10] *Vala*, 8. 270–1.

It was when Jesus said to Me,
'Thy Sins are all forgiven thee.'
The Christian trumpets loud proclaim
Thro' all the World in Jesus' name
Mutual forgiveness of each Vice,
And oped the Gates of Paradise.
The Moral Virtues in Great fear
Formed the Cross & Nails & Spear,
And the Accuser standing by
Cried out, 'Crucify! Crucify!
Our Moral Virtues ne'er can be,
Nor Warlike pomp & Majesty;
For Moral Virtues all begin
In the Accusations of Sin,
And all the Heroic Virtues End
In destroying the Sinner's Friend'.[1]

But Jesus, fearless of the consequences, 'bound old Satan in his Chain',[2] and 'Satan in his Spiritual War Drag'd at his Chariot wheels',[3] for the Christ

in his Body tight does bind
Satan & all his Hellish Crew;
And thus with wrath he did subdue
The Serpent Bulk of Nature's dross,
Till He had nail'd it to the Cross.[4]

So that

when Jesus was Crucified,
Then was perfected his glitt'ring pride:
In three Nights he devour'd his prey,
And still he devours the Body of Clay;
For dust & Clay is the Serpent's meat,
Which never was made for Man to Eat.[5]

Satan is also the 'Great Selfhood',[6] man's self-righteous pride in his own holiness, and so the Atonement consists further in the destruction of the selfhood by Jesus:

For till these terrors planted round the Gates of Eternal Life
Are driven away and annihilated, we never can repass the
Gates.[7]

[1] 'Everlasting Gospel', 2. 21–36.   [2] Ibid. b. 32.
[3] Ibid. 42, 43.   [4] Ibid. 50–4.
[5] Ibid., e. 91–6.   [6] Jerusalem, 33. 17, 18.
[7] Vala, 7a. 303–4.

It is only the Lamb of God who 'can heal This dread disease',[1] only He who can 'Annihilate the Self-hood of Deceit & False Forgiveness'.[2]

As the result of the Crucifixion, 'Satan is seen falling headlong wound round by the tail of the serpent whose bulk, nail'd to the Cross round which he wreathes, is falling into the Abyss. Sin is also represented as a female bound in one of the Serpent's folds, surrounded by her fiends. Death is Chain'd to the Cross, & Time falls together with death.'[3] Thus by the Cross not only is Satan defeated and the selfhood annihilated, but sin also is overcome—'Christ took on Sin in the Virgin's Womb & put it off on the Cross'[4]—and Jesus has taken 'away the remembrance of Sin',[5] and redeemed man from 'Error's power';[6] this is the Gospel, the 'good news of Sin and Death destroyed'.[7]

> Jesus, breaking thro' the Central Zones of Death & Hell,
> Opens Eternity in Time & Space.[8]

> Hell is open'd to Heaven: thine eyes beheld
> The dungeons burst & the Prisoners set free.[9]

This great event, which is 'a vision of the Eternal Now',[10] an incursion of the Eternal into time and space, inevitably presents the problem of the injustice of the world order, but Blake had his solution ready:

And it was enquir'd Why in a Great Solemn Assembly
The Innocent should be condemned for the Guilty. Then an Eternal
    rose,
Saying: 'If the Guilty should be condemn'd he must be an Eternal
    Death,
And one must die for another throughout all Eternity'.[11]

If the guilty were condemned at once, they would have no opportunity to work out their errors, and so would be cut off from Eternity for ever; the innocent, who cannot so be cut off, must be sacrificed on their behalf. On the Cross, Christ, 'the Lamb of God', offered Himself for man. But this is not a

[1] *Jerusalem*, 45. 15, 16.   [2] *Milton*, 18.
[3] *Last Judgment*, p. 76.   [4] *Milton*, 5. 3.
[5] *Jerusalem*, 50. 30.   [6] *Vala*, 9. 160.
[7] *Samson*.   [8] *Jerusalem*, 75. 21, 22.
[9] Ibid. 77.   [10] Lavater, 407.
[11] *Milton*, 12. 15–18.

propitiatory sacrifice, according to Blake; rather it is a perpetual example of self-sacrifice.

> unless I die thou canst not live;
> But if I die I shall rise again & thou with me.
> This is Friendship & Brotherhood: without it Man Is Not.[1]
> Wouldest thou love one who never died
> For thee, or ever die for one who had not died for thee?
> And if God dieth not for Man & giveth not himself
> Eternally for Man, Man could not exist; for Man is Love
> As God is Love: every kindness to another is a little Death
> In the Divine Image, nor can Man exist but by Brotherhood.[2]

The self-offering of Christ which was begun in eternity will continue until the consummation of all things, for every moral condemnation is a slaying of the Lamb, and at the Last Judgement each malefactor will see in his victim the Crucified Saviour, 'him whom they have pierc'd',[3] they will behold 'the blood of the Lamb slain in his Children'.[4]

Christ came that we may have life, and may have it abundantly. The death on the Cross liberated this life and now mediates it to all believers. Man, whose inner spiritual harmony was disrupted by the Fall, is now restored to wholeness, for 'Regeneration' is 'the energy of choice, the unison of various powers for one is only WILL, born under the agonies of self-denial and renounced desires'.[5]

This act of regeneration is consummated 'by the Resurrection from the dead',[6] 'by a New Spiritual birth Regenerated from Death'.[7]

> Behold Jerusalem in whose bosom the Lamb of God
> Is seen; tho' slain before her Gates, he self-renew'd remains
> Eternal, & I thro' him awake from death's dark vale.[8]

All believers are united with Christ, 'but if we died with Christ, we believe that we shall also live with him'.

> for One must be All
> And comprehend within himself all things both small & great.[9]
> the Divine Lamb . . . . . . died for all,
> And all in him died, & he put off all mortality.[10]

---

[1] *Jerusalem*, 96. 14–16.   [2] Ibid. 23–8.   [3] *Vala*, 9. 264.
[4] *Jerusalem*, 24. 2.   [5] Lavater, 20.   [6] *Vala*, 1. 19.
[7] Ibid. 9. 223.   [8] Ibid. 204–6.   [9] Ibid. 1. 286–7.   [10] Ibid. 8. 479–80.

'In Me', declared Jesus, in whom 'All dwells',[1] 'all Eternity must pass thro' condemnation and awake beyond the grave',[2] which is 'Heaven's golden Gate'.[3]

> For God himself enters Death's Door always with those that enter
> And lays down in the Grave with them, in Visions of Eternity,
> Till they awake & see Jesus & the Linen Clothes lying
> That the Females had Woven for them, & the Gates of their Father's
> House.[4]

Blake believed in the immortality of the soul, but repudiated the doctrine of the resurrection of the body. 'What is Mortality but the things relating to the Body which Dies? What is Immortality but the things relating to the Spirit which Lives Eternally?'[5] He considered that 'Every death is an improvement of the State of the Departed',[6] but it is merely like 'removing from one room to another'. The fear of death is inherent in mortality, for men are

> Terrified at Non Existence,
> For such they deem'd the death of the body.[7]

This fear is the product of Natural Religion, whose purpose is 'to impress on men the fear of death',[8] and consequently Death is 'God of All',[9] This illusion is intensified, according to Blake, by the idea of a Paradisical existence after death. Man, believing that his existence is bound up with his body, is supported in this false belief by the Church who promises the resurrection of the body.

> An Eternal Life awaits the worms of sixty winters
> In an allegorical abode where existence hath never come.[10]

This leads to a false conception of the future: 'futurity is before me like a dark lamp. Eternal death haunts all my expectations.'[11] It saps men's energies:

> O weary life! why sit I here, & give up all my powers
> To indolence, to the night of death?[12]

> O that I had never drunk the wine nor eat the bread
> Of dark mortality, or cast my view into futurity.[13]

[1] *Last Judgment*, pp. 82–4.
[2] *Jerusalem*, 35. 9, 10.
[3] 'To the Queen', 7.
[4] *Milton*, 35. 40–3.
[5] *Jerusalem*, 77.
[6] *To Linnell*, ? 1826.
[7] *Vala*, 9. 5, 6.
[8] *Milton*, 43. 38.
[9] *Vala*, 8. 331.
[10] *Europe*, 37–9.
[11] *Vala*, 3. 74, 75.
[12] Ibid. 9. 115–16.
[13] Ibid. 163–4.

The only escape from this situation lies through faith in Jesus Christ, who declares 'I am the Resurrection & the Life'.[1] 'Only believe & trust in me. Lo, I am always with thee.'[2]

> When weary Man enters his Cave
> He meets his Saviour in the Grave.[3]

For Blake, 'the Natural Body is an Obstruction to the Soul or Spiritual Body';[4] it was this Spiritual Body which Jesus revealed, thereby making evident the falsity of the rationalist view that

> that Human Form
> You call Divine is but a Worm seventy inches long
> That creeps forth in a night & is dried in the morning sun,
> In fortuitous concourse of memorys accumulated & lost.[5]

Blake maintained that on the contrary in death the covering of flesh is removed and man rises to Eternity in glory, his spiritual body being 'redeem'd to be permanent thro' Mercy Divine'.[6] In some respects this is similar to the thought of St. Paul: 'It is sown a natural body; it is raised a spiritual body. If there is a natural body, there is also a spiritual body'; but it was not the apostle's belief, nor is it that of the Church whose theology owes so much to him, that resurrection involves merely the destruction of the mortal and perishing body and the consequent liberation of the spirit. On the contrary, the orthodox teaching is that the resurrection is life restored and glorified through and by means of death; the earthly man must die completely in order to receive life. It was not that Christ 'seemed to die', but that He actually did die and rose again triumphant. It is not that man survives death, but that in and through death he rises to life again. Eternal life is possible for man, not because it is natural to his soul, but because Christ conquered the power of death and destroyed it through His resurrection. Blake was unable to perceive this truth, and although he declared that 'Plato did not bring Life & Immortality to Light. Jesus only did this';[7] his belief in the immor-

[1] *Jerusalem*, 62. 17.
[2] Ibid. 28.
[3] Gates of Paradise, 6.
[4] Berkeley, p. 218.
[5] *Jerusalem*, 33. 5–8.
[6] *Vala*, 9. 355.
[7] Berkeley, p. 214.

tality of the soul is Greek and not Biblical, Platonic and not Christian. The inconsistency of this unorthodox belief with the other elements in his system becomes clear when considered in relation to his doctrine of man, to which we now turn, for anthropology and Christology are similar to one another, since one's conception of man rests upon one's conception of Christ.

APPENDED NOTE: 'THE LAST THINGS'

Blake constantly used the language of the Last Judgement to describe an event in the life of each man, because 'whenever any Individual Rejects Error & Embraces Truth, a Last Judgment passes upon that Individual'.[1] This is strictly orthodox, for judgement is a process which takes place at every great crisis or opportunity that faces individuals or nations. Then Christ does indeed come, and men are revealed by the way they behave towards Him. But the judgement that takes place day by day looks forward to a Final Judgement, hence Blake's distinction between *a* Last Judgement and *the* Last Judgement: the former is a present experience foreshadowing the latter. 'A Last Judgment is Necessary because Fools flourish . . . this is A Last Judgment—when Men of Real Art Govern & Pretenders Fall'[1] . . . 'The Last Judgment (will be) when all those are Cast away who trouble Religion with Questions concerning Good & Evil . . . when Imagination, Art & Science & all Intellectual Gifts, all the Gifts of the Holy Ghost, are look'd upon as of no use & only Contention remains to Man, then the Last Judgment begins.'[2]

With the final consummation, all mankind will rise to eternity, both the righteous and the wicked; Blake did not believe in Hell. 'Mark that I do not believe there is such a thing (hell) litterally, but hell is the being shut up in the possession of corporeal desires which shortly weary the man, *for* ALL LIFE IS HOLY.'[3] Nevertheless, he did believe in some form of punishment. 'I know that those who are dead from the Earth, & who mocked and Despised the Meekness of True Art. . . . I know that such Mockers are Most Severely Punished in Eternity.'[4] This punishment would seem to be exclusion from the fellowship of heaven. 'Every one in Eternity will leave you, aghast at the Man who was crown'd with glory & honour by his brethren, & betray'd their cause to their enemies. You will be call'd the base Judas who betray'd his Friend!'[5] But the true followers of Christ shall meet together, each one 'a Glorified Saint who was a suffering Mortal'.[6]

> the Lamb of God Creates himself a bride & wife
> That we his Children evermore may live in Jerusalem
> Which now descendeth out of heaven, a City, yet a Woman,
> Mother of myriads redeem'd & born in her spiritual palaces,
> By a New Spiritual birth Regenerated from Death.[7]

---

[1] *Last Judgment*, pp. 82–4. [2] Ibid., p. 70.
[3] Lavater, 309. [4] *To Hayley*, 11 Dec. 1805.
[5] *To Butts*, 10 Jan. 1802. [6] *To Hayley*, 28 Dec. 1804.
[7] *Vala*, 9. 219–23.

VIII

BLAKE'S DOCTRINE OF MAN

THE Christian doctrine of man, in contrast to those modern philosophies which see him merely as the product of economic circumstances, of natural evolution, environment, or heredity, is involved and intricate; but this arises out of the very nature of man himself, for he is not a simple being, but is rather his own greatest problem. It is because Christianity refuses to omit any one facet of the truth, because it will not abstract and over-simplify, thus denying the living reality, that its teaching is so difficult to apprehend. It was his perception of this complexity that led Blake to ask 'What may Man be? who can tell!'[1] and to declare 'O what wonders are the Children of Men! Would to God that they would consider it';[2] which wonder he expressed in unforgettable words; 'O man, how great, how little thou! O man, slave of each moment, lord of eternity.'[3] By this Blake showed that he appreciated the fundamentals of the problem and saw that the tension in human existence lies in the fact that man is not only a product of nature but also of spirit; that he is not only an animal but, in a sense, a god; that he is a citizen of two worlds, in him the world of eternity and spirit meets the world of time and space. An inability to grasp this elementary truth involves a failure to understand man.

Blake's doctrine of man has already received incidental and partial consideration in reviewing the other elements in his system. Thus it has been noted that man was created by God in eternity; that 'Human nature is the image of God',[4] prior to the Fall man was the image of God, and, regenerated, he is once again called 'image of the Eternal Father'.[5] As originally created he was androgynous, but 'in the wars of Eden divided into male and female'.[6] This was the consequence of his Original Sin, when he established his own selfhood against God, and was precipitated from Eternity, to be saved from

---

[1] *Jerusalem*, 34. 25.
[2] *To Hayley*, 11 Dec. 1805.
[3] *Contemplation*.
[4] Lavater, 554.
[5] *Vala*, 9. 642.
[6] *Descriptive Catalogue*, v.

non-existence by the creation of the natural world. He possesses a free will, and, although enmeshed in matter, he is still capable of rising above it, being redeemed by Christ on the Cross, who enables man to annihilate his selfhood and has opened the way for man's immortal spirit to reascend to his eternal home.

Man will not only rise after his death in this world to a future life, but he was alive prior to his materialization; i.e. Blake accepted the idea of a pre-existent state, an idea which he used as the basis of his *Book of Thel*. It is this belief that explains his remarks in a letter to Flaxman: 'In my Brain are studies & Chambers filled with books & pictures of old, which I wrote & painted in ages of Eternity before my mortal life. . . . I look back into the regions of Reminiscence & behold our ancient days before this Earth appear'd in its vegetated mortality to my mortal vegetated Eyes.'[1] But Blake provided no further information as to the nature of this existence. Origen, who like Blake maintained a doctrine of prenatal existence, held that souls are only born into this world if they sin in that previous state, but this displaces the dogma of Original Sin, which Blake himself accepted, in favour of a series of individual and transcendental falls, of which there is no suggestion in Blake's thought. Blake, however, gave no reason why anyone should leave Eternity in order to descend into the created world, apart from hinting in one passage that it is part of the Divine Plan, and saying vaguely in another:

> And we are put on earth a little space,
> That we may learn to bear the beams of love.[2]

All that can be finally asserted of Blake's belief may be summarized in the words of Berdyaev: 'The soul is not a product of the generic process and is not created at the moment of conception, but is created by God in eternity, in the spiritual world.'[3]

On entering the world of space and time, the soul receives a body. Blake's view of the relationship between these two entities is far from clear, owing to the fact that his references to the subject group themselves into two series, of which the first apparently contradicts the second. Thus, on the one hand, he proclaimed that 'Man has no Body distinct from his soul; for

---

[1] 21 Sept. 1800.   [2] 'The Little Black Boy.'
[3] Berdyaev, *Destiny of Man*, op. cit., p. 79.

that call'd Body is a portion of Soul discern'd by the five Senses, the chief inlets of Soul in this age',[1] and that 'the notion that man has a body distinct from his soul is to be expunged'.[2] While, on the other hand, he asserted that ' "Men are born with an Angel and a Devil." This he himself interpreted as Soul and Body'; that 'the Natural Body is an Obstruction to the Soul or Spiritual Body',[3] and he besought Jesus to 'liberate us from the Natural Man',[4] who is 'at Enmity with God'.[5]

With regard to the first statements, it is possible to interpret them as expressing quite simply the Christian doctrine of the unity of body and soul, which are not independent entities but essential to each other, and are the inward and outward conditions of the same being. But Blake went farther than declaring their unity, he also affirmed their identity. In so doing he cannot be considered unorthodox. The Platonist divorce of body and soul is unacceptable to a Christian, for the form and the life are one, though distinct in function, and form to Blake is dynamic, and is an attribute of spirit, for 'Living Form is Eternal Existence'.[6]

However, if Blake were orthodox in denying a duality of body and soul, how is this to be reconciled with those statements which seem to express the opposite, the body being regarded as evil and as obstructing the activities of the soul? Moreover, how can the soul descend into the body, if the two are really one?

In his *Vision of the Last Judgment* Blake wrote: 'In Paradise they have no Corporeal & Mortal Body—that originated with the Fall & was call'd Death & cannot be removed but by a Last Judgment' (pp. 92–5). '*A* Last Judgment', as we have seen, is not an apocalyptic conception, but a present experience, for 'whenever any Individual Rejects Error & Embraces Truth, a Last Judgment passes upon that Individual' (pp. 82–4). Hence this passage indicates that it is possible to live in Paradise, even in the body, when we have rejected error—'This Man can do while in the body.'[7] We are thus led once more to Blake's distinction between the different types of vision. To the man of single vision, matter is the only reality; he is therefore unable to rise above it, and consequently it is the body that prevents

---

[1] *Marriage of Heaven and Hell*, p. 4.   [2] Ibid., p. 14.
[3] Berkeley, p. 218.   [4] Thornton, p. 3.
[5] Wordsworth, p. 3.   [6] Virgil.   [7] M.D.L.W., p. 33.

his access to the realms of the spirit; because of this, the natural body may be condemned as evil, for 'thought without affection makes a distinction between Love & Wisdom, as it does between body & spirit'.[1] Hence it was Blake's ardent desire that men 'would consider their Spiritual Life, regardless of that faint Shadow called Natural Life'.[2] However, to the man of twofold vision who 'may comprehend (spiritual things) but not the natural or external man',[3] and who, penetrating to the heart, shakes off the 'covering of Earth', the body is no longer an obstacle, it is appraised at its true worth, as that element of the soul which is visible. To speak of the descent of the soul into the body therefore is to refer to the externalization of one element of the soul which henceforth becomes corporeal and visible. The parting of soul and body at death, according to Blake, is not the discarding of something which can be utterly destroyed, but the soul's release from its visible part, or rather its ceasing to be visible. However, if Blake refused to condemn the body and its instincts, he was not always happy about its existence, and so never achieved a true synthesis of ideas on the subject, for he rejected the doctrine of the resurrection of the body which alone safeguards the unity of body and soul and indicates their true relationship.

Each man has his own distinct and eternal identity, 'Individual Identities never change nor cease.'[4] But while identities are permanent and individual, men are also one in essence, in their ultimate nature, being partakers of that 'universal human life, beyond which Nature never steps'.[5] 'Essence is not Identity, but from Essence proceeds Identity & from one Essence may proceed many Identities.'[6] It was this Essence that Blake called the Poetic Genius or the true Man, and so one can regard the universe either as one essence (the Original Man) or as many identities (men and things materialized):

contracting our infinite senses
We behold multitude, or expanding, we behold as one.[7]

The Spirit of God indwells man, for 'man is either the ark of God or a phantom of the earth & of the water',[8] and 'the

[1] M.D.L.W., p. 15.   [2] *To Hayley*, 11 Dec. 1805.
[3] M.D.L.W., pp. 8–9.   [4] *Milton*, 35. 23.
[5] *Descriptive Catalogue*, iii.   [6] M.D.L.W., p. 24.
[7] *Jerusalem*, 38. 17, 18.   [8] Lavater, 533.

Infinite alone resides in Definite & Determinate Identity'.[1]
Hence Blake could affirm 'Identities or Things are Neither
Cause nor Effect. They are Eternal',[2] so disposed by God who
'protects minute particulars every one in their own identity'.[3]
Because of his selfhood, man is unable both to unify the whole
of life and at the same time respect the identities of others;
overwhelmed by the deluge of the five senses, he does not see
that 'in every bosom a Universe expands',[4] and that 'Every
Minute Particular is Holy'.[5]

Blake criticized sense perception on four grounds. In the
first place he maintained that it is conditioned by the mind.
'Every body does not see alike. To the Eyes of a Miser a
Guinea is far more beautiful than the Sun, & a bag worn with
the use of Money has far more beautiful proportions than a
Vine filled with Grapes. The tree which moves some to tears
of joy is in the Eyes of others only a Green thing which stands in
the way.'[6] Secondly, the senses are imperfect instruments, for

> How do you know but ev'ry Bird that cuts the airy way,
> Is an immense world of delight, clos'd by your senses five?[7]

Thirdly, they are vitiated by reason, whose aim is 'to pervert all
the faculties of sense Into their own destruction'.[8] Finally,
although they are 'windows' that 'light the cavern'd Man',[9] yet
they limit and restrict man's vision, for

> Beyond the bounds of their own self their senses cannot penetrate
> As the tree knows not what is outside of its leaves & bark.[10]

This constriction was vividly expressed by Blake in verse:

> Ah weak & wide astray! Ah shut in narrow doleful form,
> Creeping in reptile flesh upon the bosom of the ground!
> The Eye of Man a little narrow orb, clos'd up & dark,
> Scarcely beholding the great light, conversing with the Void;
> The Ear a little shell, in small volutions shutting out
> All melodies & comprehending only Discord and Harmony;
> The Tongue a little moisture fills, a little food it cloys,
> A little sound it utters & its cries are faintly heard,
> Then brings forth Moral Virtue the cruel Virgin Babylon.

---

[1] *Jerusalem*, 55. 64.   [2] *Reynolds*, p. 155.   [3] *Jerusalem*, 43. 23.
[4] Ibid. 38. 49.   [5] Ibid. 69. 42.
[6] *To Trusler*, 23 Aug. 1799.   [7] *Marriage of Heaven and Hell*, p. 7.
[8] *Vala*, 8. 135-6.   [9] *Europe*, 1.   [10] *Vala*, 6. 94-5.

> Can such an Eye judge of the stars? & looking thro' its tubes
> Measure the sunny rays that point their spears in Udanadan?
> Can such an Ear, fill'd with the vapours of the yawning pit,
> Judge of the pure melodious harp struck by a hand divine?
> Can such closed Nostrils feel a joy? or tell of autumn fruits
> When grapes & figs burst their covering to the joyful air?
> Can such a Tongue boast of the living waters? or take in
> Ought but the Vegetable Ratio & loathe the faint delight?
> Can such gross Lips percieve? alas, folded within themselves
> They touch not ought, but pallid turn & tremble at every wind.[1]

Fortunately for man he possesses over and above his five senses a latent power by means of which he can communicate directly with eternity: this is the faculty of Imagination or Spiritual Sensation.

'Man brings All that he has or can have Into the World with him. Man is Born Like a Garden ready Planted & Sown. This World is too poor to produce one Seed.'[2] Amongst these aptitudes and capacities, man possesses a conscience, which may or may not be developed. 'Conscience in those that have it is unequivocal. It is the voice of God',[3] for 'no man can take darkness for light'.[4] The conscience is the 'Criterion of Moral Rectitude',[4] and virtue and honesty are its 'dictates'.[4] So certain was Blake of this that he condemned Bacon, Newton, and Locke because they

> Deny a Conscience in Man & the Communion of Saints & Angels,
> Contemning the Divine Vision & Fruition, Worshiping the Deus
> Of the Heathen, the God of This World, & the Goddess Nature.[5]

But Blake also could contend that 'Man is born a Spectre or Satan & is altogether an Evil',[6] thus apparently formulating the doctrine of total depravity, viz. that consequent upon the Fall, the image of God in man was entirely obliterated. This is an isolated statement and it is completely at variance with his usual belief, as his remark to Crabb Robinson shows; he had 'never known a very bad man who had not something very good about him'. 'Every man has a devil in him,' it is true, 'and the conflict is eternal between a man's self and God', but

---

[1] *Milton*, 5. 19–37.   [2] Reynolds, p. 157.
[3] Watson, p. 2.   [4] Ibid., p. 3.
[5] *Jerusalem*, 93. 22–4.   [6] Ibid. 52.

'Man is a twofold being, one part capable of evil & the other capable of good; . . . that which is capable of evil is also capable of good.'[1] 'Good & Evil are Qualities in Every Man, whether a Good or Evil Man.'[2] The root of this evil lies in the will, for 'there can be no Good Will. Will is always Evil.'[3] This is sound Pauline theology, for the apostle, followed by St. Augustine, insisted that while the will is free, it is yet enslaved to sin and is incapable of doing God's will. 'There is none that liveth & Sinneth not!'[4] It was Rousseau's mistake that he 'thought Men Good by Nature: he found them Evil & found no friend',[5] for sin and death entered human life with the Fall, and this issued in the destruction of order. Blake had no time for the idea that evil is merely the product of circumstances or environment. 'Want of Money & the Distress of A Thief can never be alleged as the Cause of his Thieving, for many honest people endure greater hardship with Fortitude. We must therefore seek the Cause elsewhere than in want of money, for that is the Miser's passion, not the Thief's,'[6] and Blake found it in the will.

Every man must fulfil his own potentiality, which arises from his identity. It does not matter whether according to conventional standards it is good or evil—'Every man's leading propensity ought to be call'd his leading Virtue'[7]—what is evil is hindering him in fulfilling it. This fulfilment is positive act, and 'all Act is Virtue'.[7]

It is rather surprising after Blake's emphasis on the evil in man to read Crabb Robinson's report that 'on this and other occasions he spoke as if he denied altogether the existence of evil', and to find him so minimizing sin as to declare 'What is Sin but a little Error & fault that is soon forgiven?'[8] It is, however, to be noticed that in none of his writings did Blake ever deny the existence of evil, nor even here does the diarist actually say that he did so in the course of conversation; he merely remarks that 'he spoke *as if*' he did not accept its existence. Further, Blake's under-estimation of the gravity of sin has no parallel elsewhere in his works. It is indeed the

---

[1] Lavater, 489.
[2] *Last Judgment*, pp. 86, 90.
[3] M.D.L.W., fly-leaf.
[4] *Jerusalem*, 61. 24.
[5] Ibid. 52.
[6] *To Trusler*, 23 Aug. 1799.
[7] Lavater, fly-leaf.
[8] *Jerusalem*, 20. 23–4.

opinion of one critic that sin was of no interest as a problem to
Blake, only the forgiveness of sins occupied his mind. It is true
that Blake saw in sin an opportunity for exercising the divine
power of forgiveness, to that extent sin is *felix culpa*.

> O Mercy, O Divine Humanity!
> O Forgiveness & Pity & Compassion! If I were Pure I should never
> Have known Thee: If I were Unpolluted I should never have
> Glorified thy Holiness or rejoiced in thy great Salvation.[1]

But nevertheless sin occupied an important place in his thought,
and in relation to it he elaborated his theories of Contraries
and of States.

> Man was made for Joy & Woe;
> And when this we rightly know
> Thro' the World we safely go,
> Joy & Woe are woven fine
> A Clothing for the Soul divine;
> Under every grief & pine
> Runs a joy with silken twine.[2]

'If there were no anguish,' said Boehme, 'Joy could not be
known.' Life consists of the interplay between two series of
contraries, light and darkness, life and death, good and evil.
'Without Contraries is no progression. Attraction and Repulsion, Reason and Energy, Love and Hate, are necessary to
Human existence.'[3] This idea is not peculiar to Blake, nor to
his master Boehme; it is to be found in Aristotle, in Brahman-
ism, in Traherne, and in Berdyaev; God or Brahma or Tao is
the union of these opposites—'there is a place where Contraries
are equally True.'[4]

These contraries are not mere negations.

> Contraries are Positives,
> A Negation is not a Contrary.[5]

Negations are not Contraries: Contraries mutually Exist;
But Negations Exist Not.[6]

To the logical mind the Contraries seem mutually exclusive,
but whoever attempts to 'make One Family of Contraries'[7] is

---

[1] *Jerusalem*, 61. 43–6.   [2] 'Auguries of Innocence', 56–62.
[3] *Marriage of Heaven and Hell*, p. 3.   [4] *Milton*, 33. 1.
[5] Ibid. 33.   [6] *Jerusalem*, 17. 33, 34.
[7] Ibid. 55. 15.

denying life; 'whoever tries to reconcile them seeks to destroy existence.'[1] Blake considered that every principle required for its manifestation its opposite, and hence good and evil exist together, to be finally transcended in eternity which lies beyond them.

There was one problem that the existence of evil presented most acutely to Blake's mind and that was how it is possible for a man to love his enemies. He was at first unable to appreciate this commandment of Jesus, and frankly declared 'None can see the man in the enemy; if he is ignorantly so, he is not truly an enemy; if maliciously, not a man. I cannot love my enemy, for my enemy is not man, but beast or devil, if I have any. I can love him as a beast & wish to beat him.'[2] This, of course, is not the Gospel, and Blake knew it; eventually he grasped the truth of the dictum that one should hate the sin but love the sinner. His doctrine of States is concerned with this idea. His first step was to learn from his own experience the difference between being in a temper and being possessed by anger.

> To be in a Passion you Good may do,
> But no Good if a Passion is in you.[3]

He then generalized to the effect that one must 'Distinguish therefore States from Individuals in those States. States Change, but Individual Identities never change nor cease.'[4] States are 'Combinations of Individuals'.[5] Blake considered that this doctrine was Biblical and that it was one of Jesus' appointed tasks to 'go forth to Create States, to deliver Individuals evermore!'[6] Thus

> Evil is Created into a State, that Men
> May be deliver'd time after time, evermore. Amen.
> Learn therefore . . . to distinguish the Eternal Human
> . . . from those States or Worlds in which the Spirit travels.
> This is the only means to Forgiveness of Enemies.[7]

So 'Iniquity must be imputed only To the State they are enter'd into'.[8] Although States are permanent, man is not

[1] *Marriage of Heaven and Hell*, pp. 16, 17.
[2] Lavater, 248.
[3] 'Auguries of Innocence', 111–12.
[4] *Milton*, 35. 22, 23.
[5] Ibid. 35. 10.
[6] *Jerusalem*, 35. 15, 16.
[7] Ibid. 49. 70–2, 74–5.
[8] Ibid. 49. 65–6.

bound to them. 'Man Passes on, but States remain for Ever; he passes thro' them like a traveller who may as well suppose that the places he has passed thro' exist no more, as a Man may suppose that the States he has passed thro' Exist no more.'[1] It has been said that this doctrine of States removes any idea of moral responsibility; this is, however, an untenable assertion as it depends upon man himself whether or not he enters a particular State, 'which, alas, every one on Earth is liable to enter into, & against which we should all watch'.[2] Thus Blake was able to admit the existence of evil, and condemn sin, while at the same time forgiving those who committed sins.

Blake classified men under three headings, viz. the Elect, the Reprobate, and the Redeemed. These three divisions of men 'overspread the Nations of the whole Earth',[3] and are even to be found within the confines of a single family.

> the various Classes of Men are all mark'd out determinate
> . . . & as the Spectres choose their affinities,
> So they are born on Earth, & every Class is determinate:
> But not by Natural, but by Spiritual power alone.[4]

They correspond to the 'Two Contraries & the Reasoning Negative',[5] i.e. the Elect and the Reprobate stand for the two opposed principles of life,[6] while midway between them, ill defined since they are an anomaly, are the Redeemed, who have attempted to reconcile the two contraries in their thought, being incapable of the determination necessary to belong to either the one or the other, consequently they 'live in doubts & fears'.[7]

The Elect are those who uphold the moral law; amongst their ranks therefore are to be numbered the Deists, the Pharisees, and all who adhere to the decalogue, flaunting their

---

[1] *Last Judgment*, p. 80.   [2] Ibid., pp. 76–7.
[3] *Milton*, 6. 33.   [4] Ibid. 28. 37–40.
[5] Ibid. 5. 13, 14.
[6] In *Marriage of Heaven and Hell*, the Reprobate correspond to the Devils, the Elect to the Angels, and the Redeemed are those who 'endeavour to reconcile the two' (p. 17). In Blake's mythology the Reprobate are of the class of Rintrah (*Milton*, 8. 34), i.e. wrath, those who believe that 'Energy is Eternal Delight' (*Marriage of Heaven and Hell*, p. 4); the Elect are of Satan, i.e. error (*Milton*, 12. 21); while the Redeemed are of Palamabron, i.e. pity, uncertain for 'pity divides the soul, And man unmans' (ibid. 8. 19, 20), and because they attempt to reconcile the attributes of mercy, upheld by the Reprobate, and of moral justice accepted by the Elect.
[7] Ibid. 27. 36.

'Virtues & Cruel Goodness'.[1] By their dissimulation and hypocrisy they have brought all mankind into bondage—under 'pretence to benevolence the Elect Subdu'd All'.[2] Blake scathingly remarked that they 'cannot believe in Eternal Life Except by Miracle',[3] and that their only hope of salvation, which their very self-righteousness excludes, is by 'a New Birth',[3] i.e. by undergoing that spiritual and psychical experience which was such a constant feature of the Evangelical revivalist meetings.

The Reprobate are typified by Jesus Christ Himself, who 'died as a Reprobate',[4] for they are 'form'd to destruction from the mother's womb',[5] yet they 'never cease to Believe'.[6] Hence they are to be identified with the Innocent who are condemned for the Guilty in order that the law of brotherhood and mutual forgiveness may be fulfilled.

> For the Elect cannot be Redeem'd, but Created continually
> By Offering & Atonement in the cruelties of Moral Law.[7]

Man was originally fourfold, and in eternity these three will be merged into one class, when 'Sin . . . is redeem'd in blood & fury & jealousy'.[8]

'I always thought', Blake once wrote, 'that the Human Mind was the most Prolific of All Things & Inexhaustible.'[9] This undoubted truth, made patent in the Christian doctrine of man, only serves to stimulate the desire that Blake himself had penetrated more fully and more widely into that nature, the main elements of which he so clearly grasped, and in a measure attempted to define.

[1] Ibid. 14. 34.   [2] Ibid. 27. 31.   [3] Ibid. 27. 33-4.
[4] Ibid. 14. 27.   [5] Ibid. 7. 4.   [6] Ibid. 27. 35.
[7] Ibid. 5. 11-12.   [8] *Vala*, 9. 157-8.   [9] Reynolds, p. 157.

APPENDED NOTE A: REINCARNATION

Although Blake on occasion made statements that seem to indicate a belief in reincarnation, it is difficult to see how he could have accepted such a doctrine in view of his insistence on identity and personality. Nevertheless we do find him asserting

> He touches the remotest pole, & in the center weeps
> That Man should Labour & sorrow, & learn & forget & return
> To the dark valley whence he came, to begin his labour anew.[1]

Again, John Varley, describing Blake drawing the 'Visionary Heads', records that 'the Flea told him that all fleas were inhabited by the souls of such men as were by nature blood-thirsty to excess, and were therefore providentially confined to the size and form of insects; otherwise, were he himself, for instance, the size of a horse, he would depopulate a great portion of the country'. However, the first of these statements is probably intended to emphasize the purposelessness of the idea of reincarnation, while the second evinces an underlying element of sly humour, suggesting that it should not be taken seriously.

It is unlikely that Blake did actually believe in individual reincarnation; rather he used the idea to symbolize the progressive embodiment of the collective mind in error after error as it advanced towards the light.

APPENDED NOTE B: BLAKE'S USE OF DIALECTIC

Blake's theory of Contraries requires added emphasis in view of the fact that it would appear to underlie the whole of his theology, i.e. his theology may reasonably be characterized as dialectical.

Although the dialectical method as applied to theology is closely connected at the present day with the Barthian school, its use is by no means essentially modern. It was employed by Abélard and Albertus Magnus, as well as by Luther and Calvin. To appreciate it we may turn to a phrase of Kierkegaard, who declared that 'God is infinite subjectivity'. By this statement he meant that God is never object, He is always subject. Since God is omnipresent, we cannot speak of Him in the third person, we can only address Him; just as we cannot speak *about* other people in their presence, so we cannot speak *about* God, only *to* Him. Yet if theology is to continue God must be spoken of as object, hence theology has to be dialectical. Once we forsake direct address, or prayer, our thought divides into two contrary directions, so that no one statement about God is ever entirely true unless it be corrected by another statement which seems to be its opposite. 'If you ask about God,' writes Barth, 'and if I am really to tell about him, dialectic is all that can be expected from me. . . . And therefore I have never affirmed

[1] *Vala*, 8. 569–71.

without denying and never denied without affirming, for neither affirmation nor denial can be final.'[1] This conception is of course difficult to grasp. The positive assertion sounds unambiguous and so does the negative, but the further contention that ultimately they both mean the same thing is most ambiguous; nevertheless, it is the only way in which theology can hope to approach the truth.

Blake's use of dialectic was not the same as that of Schleiermacher which seeks the mean between two opposites; such an endeavour in Blake's eyes would have involved dismissing the Contraries as negatives, whereas they are positives. Nor would Blake have agreed with Hegel who sought the synthesis beyond two opposites, which Blake would have condemned as a blasphemous attempt to 'make One Family of Contraries',[2] and so deny life, for 'whoever tries to reconcile them seeks to destroy existence'. Rather Blake would have accepted the Barthian position, which endeavours to go back to the original state from which the Contraries arose—'there is a place where Contraries are equally true'.[3] 'The truth lies not in the Yes and not in the No but in the knowledge of the beginning from which the Yes and the No arise';[4] or in more philosophical language: 'the great negative precedes the small one, as it precedes the small positive. The original is the synthesis. It is out of this that both thesis and antithesis arise.'[5]

Once we have accepted the idea that Blake's theology is dialectical, that his theory of Contraries applies not only to life in general but to his thought in particular, it becomes easier of appreciation. We now see that his thought progresses by thesis and antithesis; thus he rejects the reality of nature only to counter this by asserting its abiding value; he condemns the body and then declares its identity with the soul; he repudiates the law and at the same time appreciates its importance; he looks upon sin as a barrier to communion, but equally he views it as an occasion for exercising forgiveness; he believes in Creation as an act of mercy, but regards it as a consequence of the Fall; he discourses on the immanence of God and yet acknowledges His transcendence—and at the beginning and end of it all is God, the Divine Humanity, the *coincidentia oppositorum*.

[1] K. Barth, *The Word of God and the Word of Man*, 1928, p. 209.
[2] *Jerusalem*, 55. 15.   [3] *Milton*, 33. 1.
[4] Barth, op. cit., p. 73.   [5] Barth, op. cit., p. 299.

IX

BLAKE'S ETHICS

ALTHOUGH it has to be admitted that Blake's theology is, at the most, uneven and fragmentary, yet there is one feature of it which he expounded in far more detail than any other. He grasped, as few men before or since have succeeded in doing, the essential nature of Christian ethics, and so vital did he consider this insight to be that he devoted much of his time and tireless energy to proclaiming it. All his Prophetic books, most of his lyrical poems, and the majority of his letters contain references to it. Here was one element of Christianity that he penetrated to the core; this was one theme that he never tired of reaffirming. This message, to which his contemporaries turned a deaf ear, if indeed they could ever have understood it, and to which not only the people of Blake's day but those of all ages are persistently blind, this message is identical with the teaching of St. Paul: 'with freedom did Christ set us free', for 'Christ redeemed us from the curse of the law, having become a curse for us'.

Christ was a revolutionary, so much so that even to-day people wilfully misinterpret His words and explain them away rather than accept their challenge. Christ turned the moral ideas of the Jews upside down, and it was because the Church of the eighteenth century failed to realize this that Blake complained bitterly that they were crucifying Christ 'with the Head Downwards'.[1]

Christ declared that the ethics of the law issue in self-righteousness, for it is man alone who thereby achieves his own perfection. Outward rules of morality are useless, since a man may observe them faithfully and yet inwardly be filled with pride, envy, and self-love. Such ethics are essentially anthropocentric, since everything revolves round man's personal happiness and moral rectitude, i.e. around himself. The Pharisees were righteous, and according to their own lights they were good; it is nonsense to think otherwise; they did fulfil the law,

---

[1] *Last Judgment*, p. 87.

down to the last detail; they were not 'extortioners, unjust, adulterers', they fasted 'twice in the week', and they gave tithes of all that they had; but their righteousness was that of a legalistic ethic and therefore a self-righteousness.

Such legalism is un-freedom, since the good done from a sense of duty is never the good, for merely to obey due to a sense of unwilling constraint is bondage—the bondage of sin. Consequently, the basis of legalism is to be found in the Fall, in the fact that man has fallen away from union with God. The Crucifixion was the work of the highest form of ethical righteousness. Jesus was condemned for blasphemy, and the Pharisees were utterly and entirely sincere in believing that His death was essential to save morality. Thus the curse of legalism is revealed by the Cross. Christian ethics are not the ethics of law but of redemption, for Christianity is the revelation of grace. Legalistic ethics are social, not personal and individual, they organize the life of the herd, but neglect the creative human personality which rises above the common level. But conduct directed by abstract principles can never be good. There are no abstract moral norms, recognized by Christianity, to be applied to all situations; each problem demands its own individual solution as it arises. The only Good is obedient behaviour, not to the law, but to the sovereign will of God. The Good consists in doing God's will. Hence, as the will of God is free, the Christian is also free, under the personal orders of God. This is Christianity, the religion of liberty; it was also the faith of William Blake, the prophet of freedom.

'The Gospel', according to Blake, 'is Forgiveness of Sins & has No Moral Precepts; these belong to Plato & Seneca & Nero.'[1] That is to say, 'if Morality was Christianity, Socrates was The Saviour.'[2] Hence, he asserted 'Christ came not to call the Virtuous',[3] and he posed the rhetorical question, 'Does God love the Righteous according to the Gospel, or does he not cast them off?'[4]

Blake was constantly attacking all moral codes, and made a different accusation every time he set out to castigate them. At one time he declared that they kill all joy, which is 'perverted to ten commands',[1] and they are frustrating because they are impossible of faithful fulfilment.

> No individual can keep these Laws, for they are death
> To every energy of man and forbid the springs of life.[2]

'No flesh nor spirit could keep' these 'iron laws one moment'.[3] They demand the impossible and take vengeance for failure, so that men become 'trembling victims of . . . Moral Justice'.[4] Again, legalistic ethics are inspired by a love of punishment and vengeance and kill all imaginative activity. They are 'a Scheme of Human conduct invisible & incomprehensible',[5] which promotes harshness and repression.

> Every house a den, every man bound: the shadows are fill'd
> With spectres, and the windows wove over with curses of iron:
> Over the doors 'Thou shalt not,' & over the chimneys 'Fear' is
>   written.[6]
> All Love is lost: Terror succeeds, & Hatred instead of Love,
> And stern Demands of Right & Duty instead of Liberty.[7]

Moral codes have no consideration for the individual, they know nothing of the inner man, and merely regulate the life of the outer man in relation to society. 'How ridiculous it would be', contended Blake, 'to see the Sheep Endeavouring to walk like the Dog, or the Ox striving to trot like the Horse; just as Ridiculous as it is to see One Man Striving to Imitate Another. Man varies from Man more than Animal from Animal of different Species.'[8] Hence 'One Law for the Lion & Ox is Oppression'.[9]

> Why is one law given to the lion & the patient Ox?
> Dost not thou see that men cannot be formed all alike?[10]

The careful balance of duty against duty, characteristic of the law, is absurd, for

> How can one joy absorb another? are not different joys
> Holy, eternal, infinite? and each joy is a Love?[11]

[1] *America*, 61.
[2] *Jerusalem*, 35. 11–12.
[3] *Book of Urizen*, viii. 4.
[4] *Jerusalem*, 23. 34.
[5] *Milton*, 4. 13.
[6] *Europe*, 132–4.
[7] *Vala*, 1. 32–3.
[8] Reynolds, p. 149.
[9] *Marriage of Heaven and Hell*, p. 24.
[10] *Tiriel*, 8. 9, 10.
[11] *Daughters of Albion*, 116, 117.

All moralism issues in hypocrisy, an attitude which Blake depicted in biting terms:

> Listen to the Words of Wisdom,
> So shall (you) govern over all: let Moral Duty tune your tongue,
> But be your hearts harder than the nether millstone.
>
> .   .   .   .
>
> Compell the poor to live upon a Crust of bread, by soft mild arts.
> Smile when they frown, frown when they smile; & when a man looks pale
>   pale
> With labour & abstinence, say he looks healthy & happy;
> And when his children sicken, let them die; there are enough
> Born, even too many, & our Earth will be overrun
> Without these arts. If you would make the poor live with temper(ance),
> With pomp give every crust of bread you give; with gracious cunning
> Magnify small gifts; reduce the man to want a gift, & then give with
>   pomp.
> Say he smiles if you hear him sigh. If pale, say he is ruddy.
> Preach temperance: say he is overgorg'd & drowns his wit
> In strong drink, tho' you know that bread & water are all
> He can afford. Flatter his wife, pity his children, till we can
> Reduce all to our will, as spaniels are taught with art.[1]

Finally, the moral law inculcates self-righteousness, which was revealed once and for all by the Crucifixion of Jesus. 'He who does Forgive Sin is Crucified as an Abettor of Criminals, & he who performs Works of Mercy in Any Shape whatever is punish'd &, if possible, destroy'd, not thro' envy or Hatred or Malice, but thro' Self Righteousness that thinks it does God service, which God is Satan.'[2] 'Natural Morality or Self-Righteousness', affirmed Blake, 'was the Religion of the Pharisees who murder'd Jesus. Deism is the same & ends in the same.'[3] Jesus, according to Blake, did indeed reveal 'the curse of the law'.

The conception of moral virtue is also derived from the law, which attempts to make man an automaton of virtue. Once virtue ceases to be regarded as the product of divine action, it becomes a mere human acquisition. Further, once 'being good' is conceived of as a human quality, then it follows that there are a number of such virtues. The Good is then split asunder and

---

[1] *Vala*, 7a. 111–13, 118–30.   [2] *Last Judgment*, pp. 92–5.
[3] *Jerusalem*, 52.

man possesses not one quality, but several: not one virtue, but many. The Good, which is one, is divided into little pieces, a system of virtues is introduced, and the conception of the Good is completely externalized. Then it is that virtue becomes dried up and formal, deprived of any gracious life-giving energy. Virtue becomes individualistic and anthropocentric, and issues, like all legalism, in self-righteousness. So it was that the author of the *Mirror of Simple Souls* declared: 'Virtues, I take my leave of you for evermore,' and Blake considered the seven virtues as forms of spiritual disease, and spoke of 'Temperance, Prudence, Justice, Fortitude, the four pillars of tyranny'.[1] 'Moral Virtues do not Exist; they are Allegories & dissimulations.'[2] In religion the fine distinctions between the virtues are disregarded and they are all gathered into one supreme quality of love. So Blake believed that 'Jesus was all virtue, and acted from impulse, not from rules'.[3]

It was the Crucifixion again which, in Blake's judgement, revealed the falsity of the moral virtues; which 'are continual Accusers of Sin & promote Eternal Wars & Dominency over others'.[4] Jesus was condemned because of

> the sneaking Pride of Heroic Schools,
> And the Scribes' & Pharisees' Virtuous Rules.[5]

Hence Blake could say

> The Moral Virtues in Great Fear
> Formed the Cross & Nails & Spear.[6]

The Pharisees realized that their whole edifice of law and moral virtue was in jeopardy because of Jesus' teaching; they knew that if He were allowed to continue unchecked

> Our Moral Virtues ne'er can be,
> Nor Warlike pomp & Majesty;
> For Moral Virtues all Begin
> In the Accusations of Sin,
> And all the Heroic Virtues End
> In destroying the Sinners' Friend.[7]

---

[1] *Milton*, 31. 49. [2] *Last Judgment*, p. 91.
[3] *Marriage of Heaven and Hell*, p. 23.
[4] Berkeley, p. 215. [5] 'Everlasting Gospel', d. 27, 28.
[6] Ibid. 2. 27, 28. [7] Ibid. 2. 31–6.

What they did not realize was that by crucifying Jesus they
were only making their own self-righteousness more apparent,
for 'then was perfected his glitt'ring pride'.[1]

Blake's perspicacity is amazing; with no one to guide him,
and with the contemporary Church herself, infected with
Deism, teaching natural morality, by his own efforts he reached
the core of the Gospel, and by his innate genius expounded it in
immortal words. 'There is not one Moral Virtue that Jesus
Inculcated but Plato & Cicero did Inculcate before him;
what then did Christ Inculcate? Forgiveness of Sins. This
alone is the Gospel, & this is the Life & Immortality brought
to light by Jesus.'[2]

> If Moral Virtue was Christianity,
> Christ's Pretensions were all Vanity,
> And Cai(a)phas & Pilate, Men
> Praise Worthy, & the Lion's Den
> And not the Sheepfold, Allegories
> Of God & Heaven & their Glories.
> The Moral Christian is the Cause
> Of the Unbeliever & his Laws.
> The Roman Virtues, Warlike Fame,
> Take Jesus' & Jehovah's Name;
> For what is Antichrist but those
> Who against Sinners Heaven close
> With Iron bars, in Virtuous State,
> And Rhadamanthus at the Gate?[3]

Despite all this, the law has a part to play. It is necessary
because a man cannot depend upon the inner perfection of his
neighbour. The paradox of law is that it does not know the
living personality, and yet at the same time it protects it from
interference by others. Blake, for all his condemnation of moral
codes, perceived this quite clearly. 'Laws', he said, 'were made
to keep fair play.'[4] 'You cannot have Liberty in this World
without what you call Moral Virtue, & you cannot have Moral
Virtue without the Slavery of that half of the Human Race who
hate what you call Moral Virtue.'[5] Blake thus showed that he
realized that the law is not sin, but that sin has given rise to it

[1] Ibid. e. 92.   [2] Ibid., introduction.
[3] Ibid. 1.   [4] 'Blind-Man's Buff', 70.
[5] *Last Judgment*, 92–5.

and is manifested by it. Moral codes are merely 'laws of prudence' which have been called 'the eternal Laws of God',[1] and while necessary to social life, the individual has been set free from them by Christ, and so Blake gave his solemn warning: 'Man is the ark of God`. . . if thou seekest by human policy to guide this ark, remember Uzzah, 11 Saml vi. ch.'[2]

As the source of the Good is God, and as man is only good not by reason of virtuous acts but by living in the love of God, Blake could maintain that 'Energy is Eternal Delight',[3] and that 'the soul of sweet delight can never be defil'd'.[4] 'Exuberance is Beauty',[5] so 'Damn braces. Bless relaxes.'[4] 'Men are admitted in Heaven not because they have curbed & govern'd their Passions or have no Passions, but because they have Cultivated their Understandings.'[6] 'Those who are cast out (of heaven) are All Those who, having no Passions of their own because No Intellect, Have spent their lives in Curbing & Governing other People's by the Various arts of Poverty & Cruelty of all kinds.'[7] 'The Treasures of Heaven' indeed 'are not Negations of Passion, but Realities of Intellect, from which all the Passions Emanate Uncurbed in their Eternal Glory.'[7] Thus 'Enjoyment & not Abstinence is the food of Intellect',[8] for 'every thing that lives is holy'.[9] This led Blake to the exaggerated statement, which yet possesses an element of truth: 'Active Evil is better than Passive Good,'[10] for 'all Act is Virtue',[11] and 'Thought is act'.[12]

If we turn now to certain concrete problems of ethics, it should not be with any expectation of discovering rules and casuistic reasonings; rather we shall find Blake's own personal and creative solutions of the moral questions that presented themselves to him.

The problem to which Blake gave most attention was that of sex. This was not because he was highly erotic by nature, but because he considered that the evil working of the moral law

[1] *Book of Urizen*, ix. 5.
[2] Lavater, 533.
[3] *Marriage of Heaven and Hell*, p. 4.
[4] Ibid., p. 9.
[5] Ibid., p. 10.
[6] *Last Judgment*, p. 87.
[7] Ibid., p. 87.
[8] *To Cumberland*, 6 Dec. 1795.
[9] *Daughters of Albion*, 215.
[10] Lavater, 409.
[11] Ibid., fly-leaf.
[12] Bacon.

is nowhere so evident than in the effects it has upon love, which
it vitiates or corrupts.

> I saw the limbs form'd for exercise contemn'd, & the beauty of
> Eternity look'd upon as deformity, & loveliness as a dry tree.[1]

> a Man dare hardly to embrace
> His own Wife for the terrors of Chastity that they call
> By the name of Morality.[2]

The law represses love so that it finds an outlet in lust.

> Pitying I wept to see the woe
> That Love & Beauty undergo,
> To be consum'd in burning Fires
> And in ungratified desires.[3]

Men 'shiver in religious caves beneath the burning fires of lust',[4]
and youth pines away with desire. The ethics of legalism produce inhibitions and impurity of mind, which results in self-
abuse:

> The moment of desire! the moment of desire! The virgin
> That pines for man shall awaken her womb to enormous joys
> In the secret shadows of her chamber: the youth shut up from
> The lustful joy shall forget to generate & create an amorous image
> In the shadows of his curtains and in the folds of his silent pillow.
> Are not these the places of religion, the rewards of continence,
> The self enjoyings of self denial? why dost thou seek religion?
> Is it because acts are not lovely that thou seekest solitude
> Where the horrible darkness is impressed with reflections of desire?[5]

So love is regarded as a sin,

> Children of the future Age
> Reading this indignant page,
> Know that in a former time,
> Love! sweet Love! was thought a crime.[6]

Love has become a matter of law and outward observance, but
this is a travesty of the truth, for

> pale religious letchery, seeking Virginity,
> May find it in a harlot, and in coarse-clad honesty
> The undefil'd, tho' ravished in her cradle night and morn.[7]

---

[1] *Jerusalem*, 9. 7, 8.   [2] Ibid. 36. 44–6.   [3] 'The Golden Net.'
[4] *Daughters of Albion*, 32, 33.   [5] Ibid. 178–86.
[6] 'A Little Girl Lost.'   [7] *America*, 68–70.

Purity cannot be comprehended in a legal definition, it depends
upon the disposition of the spirit within. Love is, or should be,
free.

> I cry: Love! Love! Love! happy, happy Love! free as the mountain
>   wind!
> Can that be love that drinks another as a sponge drinks water,
> That clouds with jealousy his nights, with weepings all the day?[1]

The marriage bond is a tyranny, for 'she who burns with youth,
and knows no fixed lot, is bound In spells of law to one she
loaths',[2] and man is 'bound in sorrow whose ev'ry function is
fill'd with its fiery desire'.[3] The consequence is that love has
become a source of hypocrisy and dissembling; women 'catch
virgin joy And brand it with the name of whore, & sell it in the
night',[4] and 'from her childhood shall the little female Spread
nets in every secret path'.[5]

If Christianity be liberty, asked Blake, how can it sanction
the mortifying legal union of man and woman? The steps he
took to arrive at a solution of this problem are traced for us in
the Rossetti MS.[6]

The first poem reveals that Blake had rejected the offer of
love by another woman and had disclosed the fact to his wife,
who reacted to his confidence with jealousy and thereby
shattered their innocent romantic joy. This led him to declare
that it is useless to proclaim one's love; it is not a matter for
speech, but for instinct, and he bitterly concluded that love in
any case is selfish and grasping. What food is there for the
spirit in earthly love? If this be marriage, what of those who
are excluded from it? But surely, Blake continued, married love
is beautiful? and then he sadly answered himself that it is
deformed by man-made conventions. This seems to leave no

---

[1] *Daughters of Albion*, 191–3.   [2] Ibid. 132–3.
[3] *French Revolution*, 184–5.   [4] *Daughters of Albion*, 163–4.   [5] *Europe*, 40–1.
[6] As the poems in the Rossetti MS. are not printed by Keynes in the order in
which Blake jotted them down, I give here the titles of the poems in the order
which I have used (for a fuller development of the thought of this manuscript see
J. Wicksteed, *Blake's Innocence and Experience*, 1928, pp. 214–80): i. 'My Pretty Rose
Tree'; ii. 'Never seek to tell thy love'; iii. 'The Clod and the Pebble'; iv. 'I laid me
down upon a bank'; v. 'The Garden of Love'; vi. 'I saw a chapel all of gold';
vii. 'I fear'd the fury of my wind'; viii. 'Infant sorrow'; ix. 'Silent, silent night'; x.
'In a Mirtle Shade'; xi. 'To Nobodaddy'; xii. 'The Marriage Ring'; xiii. 'The
sword sung on the barren heath'; xiv. 'In a wife I would desire'; xv. 'He who
binds to himself a joy'; xvi. 'What is it men in women require?'

other course open than that of frank bestiality, but even this is no solution. He then decided that the only thing to do is to refrain from avowals of love, and content oneself with passively radiating it; but this unselfish offering only meets with rebuff, for everyone has selfish ends in love. The pleasures of sex are condemned on all sides, especially by the priests, who yet indulge secretly in them, so Blake wondered how one could ever expect perfect happiness when all the joys of love are cloaked in pretence. Nevertheless, he was sure that love must be free:

> Love, free love, cannot be bound
> To any tree that grows on ground.[1]

But he was compelled to admit that it is in bondage, and hence he was prompted to ask who was responsible for it; he rejected the idea that it is due to any divine commands, and laid the blame upon women and the jealousy of innocence waking to adolescence. But at last, in a flash, he saw that the only condition in which love may be enjoyed in peace and security is in the circle of wedded love, and that the law cannot defeat love, though it may devastate it at times. So he was able to reconcile desire with the love of a wedded wife, as long as there is no selfishness between the couple, only mutual joy.

Blake, of course, had not really solved the problem, for marriage by its very nature is not only individual but social, and as such it comes within the scope of the law which regulates the life of the herd. Even the Christian cannot avoid the law here, nor even if he could would he do so for the sake of those who need it. From the point of view of redemption all human marriage is questionable and is of a provisional character, since 'in the resurrection they neither marry nor are given in marriage'. Yet a distinction must be drawn between marriage founded upon love and freedom, and marriage as a legal and economic institution determined by social conventions. Marriage in the former sense is a sacrament, but only if based upon real love, not upon a passing infatuation. The sacrament of marriage is not social, for love is not something that can be regulated from outside. It is only this personal love in freedom enjoyed by mutual consent that can liberate man from sexual lust.

[1] 'In a Mirtle Shade.'

It is here that a further complicating factor enters the problem, viz. the family. Whereas love in marriage may be a means of transcending the selfhood, in so far as either person is compelled to admit the eternal validity and being of the other, yet, as Blake saw, the family may become an extension of the selfhood.

> Is this thy soft Family-Love,
> Thy cruel Patriarchal pride,
> Planting thy Family alone,
> Destroying all the World beside?[1]

The family may well be an obstacle to spiritual progress, in so far as in order to support it man frequently becomes immersed in financial and other material concerns, because money is 'the life's blood of Poor Families'.[2] Hence

> A man's worst enemies are those
> Of his own house & family;
> And he who makes his law a curse,
> By his own law shall surely die.[3]

But, at the same time, the family is a school of sacrifice, and so Blake could write to his friend Linnell: 'You have a Family, I have none; there is no comparison between our necessary avocations.'[4]

The sacramental aspect of the sex act is only hinted at by Blake, but he did look upon sex, or the sense of touch which he regarded as identical with it, as a means of entrance into eternity—'Thro' one (sense) himself pass out what time he please.'[5] This would appear to be rendered possible by the fact that in and through sexual intercourse man and woman are united in one androgynous image, thus restoring, if only for a moment, the original condition and wholeness of unfallen man. The sex act then is a mutual fulfilment, re-creating the initial harmony of creation. This union is only perfected in God, whose Spirit thereby descends to earth, that they may ascend to heaven. It thus partakes of a sacramental nature, mediating grace and inspiration to the soul.

A second moral problem that exercised Blake's mind, though by no means to such an extent as sex and marriage, was that of

---

[1] *Jerusalem*, 27.   [2] Laocoon.   [3] *Jerusalem*, 27.
[4] 5 July 1826.   [5] *Europe*, 5.

war. Briefly his solution was pacifism, but he only reached this conviction after several years of indecision.

In his first poems Blake made it clear that he believed that some wars are justifiable, especially those waged against tyranny, but those conducted in the interests of despots are indefensible, although at the same time he was far from glorifying war, which he regarded as despicable. However, with such views it was natural for him to be an ardent supporter of the French Revolution, and he was to be seen walking the streets of London with the *bonnet rouge*, the symbol of liberty, firmly planted upon his head. But the September massacres, the rise of Napoleon, and the war between France and Great Britain disillusioned the 'Liberty Boy', who became more and more a hater of war, until at last he refused to admit that any war could ever be justified. 'God never makes one man murder another, nor one nation.'[1]

> the hapless Soldier's sigh
> Runs in blood down Palace walls.[2]

He saw the seeds of this strife in legalistic religion which exacts a penalty for non-compliance with its rules and preaches vengeance instead of forgiveness, so 'the priest promotes war & the soldier peace'.[3] 'War is energy Enslav'd.'[4]

> Nought can deform the Human Race
> Like to the Armour's iron brace.[5]

Nor, according to Blake, is there anything to be gained by waging war, it can never improve the condition of any State. 'The increase of a State, as of a man, is from internal improvement or intellectual acquirement. Man is not improved by the hurt of another. States are not improved at the expense of foreigners.'[6] War is an extension of the selfhood; it is the product of the conflict that arises from the clash of wills in fallen egocentric man; accordingly war can never be eradicated from human history by means of itself, the only way is love.

> But vain the Sword & vain the Bow,
> They never can work War's overthrow.
> The Hermit's Prayer & the Widow's tear
> Alone can free the World from fear.[7]

---

[1] Watson, p. 6.   [2] 'London', 3.   [3] 'The Human Image', 7.
[4] *Vala*, 9. 151.   [5] 'Auguries of Innocence', 99, 100.
[6] Bacon.   [7] 'The Grey Monk', 7.

Blake's pacifism, with its underlying note of forbearance and forgiveness, has as its counterpart the doctrine of individual forgiveness. In the same way that his ideas on war gradually changed, so his conception of forgiveness developed.

At first he considered that forgiveness should only be given if the offender were prepared to alter his ways, 'never forgive him till he mends'.[1] 'Forgiveness of enemies can only come upon their repentance.'[2] 'The public seldom forgive twice', wrote Lavater,[3] and Blake's comment was 'let us take their example'. 'Severity of judgment is a great virtue,' he maintained.[4] This was a different Blake to the one who to Crabb Robinson 'declared against those who sat in judgment on others', and who affirmed that 'the Glory of Christianity is To Conquer by Forgiveness',[5] which should be free and unconditional. Blake saw that it is impossible to condemn a man for his actions, since one cannot know his motives.

But go! merciless man! enter into the infinite labyrinth of another's brain
Ere thou measure the circle that he shall run.[6]

A man can outwardly appear generous and high-principled, and yet his conduct may arise entirely from self-righteousness; on the other hand, a man may seem haughty and amoral, and yet he may be truly humble and entirely chaste. There is only one way in which man may live the life of love, viz. 'Giving, recieving, and forgiving each other's trespasses.'[7]

Man liveth not by Self alone, but in his brother's face
Each shall behold the Eternal Father & love & joy abound.[8]

for 'man subsists by Brotherhood & Universal Love',[9] and

Mutual Forgiveness of each Vice
Such are the Gates of Paradise.[10]

Milton, Jerusalem, and *The Ghost of Abel* are almost wholly devoted to the exposition of the forgiveness of sins, the various episodes being used to illustrate its practice; for 'without For-

[1] Lavater, 477.
[2] Ibid. 401.
[3] Ibid. 606.
[4] Ibid. 36.
[5] *Jerusalem,* 52.
[6] *French Revolution,* 192–3.
[7] *Jerusalem,* 38. 22.
[8] *Vala,* 9. 639–40.
[9] Ibid. 636.
[10] *Gates of Paradise,* prologue.

giveness of Sin, Love is Itself Eternal Death'.[1] Christianity is
the forgiveness of sins, 'the Spirit of Jesus is continual forgiveness
of Sin: he who waits to be righteous before he enters into the
Saviour's kingdom, the Divine Body, will never enter there.'[2]
In 'a World in which Man is by his Nature the Enemy of Man'[3]
Blake was not so isolated as to imagine that this would be easy.

> In Heaven the only Art of Living
> Is Forgetting & Forgiving:
> But if you on Earth Forgive,
> You shall not find where to Live.[4]

In particular, he found it difficult to forgive those of his friends
whom he thought, rightly or wrongly, to have done him some
harm. 'It is easier to forgive an Enemy than to forgive a Friend,'[5]
for not infrequently 'Corporeal Friends are Spiritual Enemies',[6]
who

> do unkind things in kindness, with power arm'd to say
> The most irritating things in the midst of tears and love.[7]

Nevertheless, 'the cut worm forgives the plow',[8] and however
hard it may be to practise forgiveness, it is the only path that
leads to universal harmony, for 'he who will not comingle in
Love must be adjoin'd by Hate';[9] but it is a path that calls for
continual acts of self-sacrifice. 'Jehovah's Salvation is without
Money & without Price, in the Continual Forgiveness of Sin.'[10]

> And this is the Covenant
> Of Jehovah: If you Forgive one-another, so shall Jehovah Forgive
> You
> That He Himself may Dwell among You.[11]

Although the conception of virtues, as we have seen, atomizes
and externalizes the Good, yet in the New Testament we do find
reference made to the several virtues, and it is from St. Paul
that the Church has derived her three theological virtues,
which, with the cardinal virtues, Blake condemned as seven
diseases of the soul. If the previous argument were correct,

---

[1] *Jerusalem*, 64. 24.
[2] Ibid. 3.
[3] Ibid. 43. 52.
[4] Ibid. 81.
[5] Ibid. 91. 1.
[6] *Milton*, 4. 26.
[7] Ibid. 12. 32–3.
[8] *Marriage of Heaven and Hell*, p. 7.
[9] *Jerusalem*, 66. 56.
[10] Ibid. 61. 21, 22.
[11] Ibid. 61. 24–6.

however, then the New Testament writers must have been using the categories of virtues to suggest that in them is exhibited the various forms of the one life in love. Thus the only Good is living in love, but this life appears in a variety of ways in connexion with the life of others; a particular virtue is only the special way in which one person takes another into account. Virtues then do not arise from the self, but derive from the coexistence of human beings, and therefore they are not positive in character. Yet when this has been said, it must not be forgotten that whereas the *person* cannot be conceived in terms of qualities, the *character* may be. In this sense, virtues do exist as qualities in persons. Blake, with his strong belief in divine guidance and inspiration, rejected all idea of virtue as something man can acquire, but attempted to transvalue the separate virtues in order to set them in their true light as given qualities. The only virtue with which he dealt with at all fully in this way was humility, but even here his transvaluation is apparent not so much in exposition as in living, and his ideas have to be gathered from statements which bear on the subject without being actually concerned directly with it.

At the outset it would seem quite certain that Blake was entirely lacking in humility. 'Excessive pride', said Crabb Robinson, 'equally denoted Blake and Barry.' This judgement appears to derive some support from the claims which Blake made for his artistic achievements. To his friend and patron Butts, Blake wrote: 'The Pictures which I painted for you Are Equal in Every part of the Art, and superior in One to anything that has been done since the age of Rafael.'[1] In his *Public Address*, which was never published, he declared 'this Print is the Finest that has been done or is likely to be done in England' (pp. 24–5). In his *Descriptive Catalogue*, which was printed and circulated, describing his painting of the Ancient Britons, he asserted that 'he defies competition in colouring' (v). And yet Blake was truly humble!

Humility is generally taken to describe the relationship of man with man; it is, according to this way of thinking, primarily man-centred; but to the Christian, humility describes man's relationship to God. The falsely humble man is he who thinks little of himself, the truly humble man is he who does not think

[1] 22 Nov. 1802.

of himself at all because he is thinking of God. So humility
may be defined as a just estimate of our own value. Hence it
does not imply doubt of a man's powers, but a right understanding of their nature. Thus Dürer could write to one who
had found fault with his work: 'It cannot be better done'; and
Blake could say, 'If a man is a master of his profession, he cannot
be ignorant that he is so,'[1] and 'I do not pretend to Paint better
than Rafael or Mich. Angelo or Julio Romano or Alb. Durer,
but I do Pretend to Paint finer than Rubens or Rembt. or
Correggio or Titian'.[2] Blake was a genius and he knew it; but
he also knew that this was not a cause for pride; what he was,
what he did, all his artistic creation, was really the work of a
higher power operating through him. He did not claim to be
'any other than the Secretary' of his poems.[3] Of his paintings
and designs, he wrote 'tho' I call them Mine, I know that they
are not Mine',[4] words which he also applied to the songs he
sang to his wife on his death-bed. 'He knows that what he does
is not inferior to the grandest Antiques. Superior they cannot
be, for human power cannot go beyond either what he does, or
what they have done'—but this is not the end, he continued—
'it is the gift of God, it is inspiration and vision . . . the human
mind cannot go beyond the gift of God, the Holy Ghost.'[5] 'It is
part of our duty to God & man', he told Butts, 'to take due care
of his Gifts; & tho' we ought not (to) think *more* highly of ourselves, yet we ought to think *As* highly of ourselves as immortals
ought to think.'[6] To all those who have condemned Blake of
lacking in humility he gave his own reply: 'He who despises &
mocks a Mental gift in another, calling it pride & selfishness
& sin, mocks Jesus the giver of every Mental Gift.'[7]

From the day when, as a young man, he penned the words:
'Lo then, Humility, take it, and wear it in thine heart; lord of
thyself thou then art lord of all',[8] to the day when he described
the City of Art whose floors are humility, and until his death,
Blake lived the life of a truly humble man—'Humble to God,
Haughty to Man'[9]—ready to admit his mistakes—'I do not
pretend to be Perfect',[10] not seeking earthly fame, content in his

[1] *Descriptive Catalogue*, xvi.
[2] *Public Address*, p. 57.
[3] *To Butts*, 6 July, 1803.
[4] *To Trusler*, 16 Aug. 1799.
[5] *Descriptive Catalogue*, v.
[6] 10 Jan. 1802.
[7] *Jerusalem*, 77.
[8] *Contemplation*.
[9] 'Everlasting Gospel', d. 63.
[10] *To Butts*, 22 Nov. 1802.

work of which he knew himself a master, for 'Can a Poet doubt the Visions of Jehovah?'[1] He had no time for false humility, for 'what are all crawlers but mimickers of humility & love?'[2] 'Your humility', said Lavater (573), 'is equal to your desire of being unnoticed, unobserved in your acts of virtue.' Blake underlined this aphorism, and added the comment 'True humility'. True humility makes no show of being humble, it seeks only to hide itself. Such was Blake, a man who knew his own gifts and appraised them at their true worth, refusing to deny them because to do so would have been to blaspheme the Holy Ghost; a man who showed no slave mentality, but who was a worthy guardian of the treasure of his nature.

In his works Blake outlined few ethical problems, partly perhaps because he did not want his readers to embody his personal solutions into another law, and partly because morality is a question of living and not of theory, of freedom and not of regulation. Nevertheless, he wrote sufficient on the subject to make it evident that few men before or since have so clearly understood the revolutionary nature of Christian ethics.

[1] *Ghost of Abel*, 2.   [2] Lavater, 71.

APPENDED NOTE: BLAKE'S 'HYPOCRISY'

While the truth or falsity of a theory does not depend upon the personality of its exponent, just as the truth or falsity of the Gospel is not affected by the failure of individual Christians to live up to its claims, so Blake's ethic would not stand condemned if it could be shown that he did not practise what he preached. Yet the charge of hypocrisy made against him requires investigation, since, if it be correct, not only is his personal integrity impaired, but the whole of his system lies under suspicion, for there is no reason to suppose that a hypocrite means what he says or writes.

The general impression that Blake was two-faced, and relieved his feelings by writing epigrams and disguised his true attitude, is supported by Harold Bruce in his book *William Blake in this World* (1925, p. 99), where he prints the epigrams about and the letters to Hayley side by side, the one being 'overtones', the other 'conventional words'. But there is no indication at all that the letters were written at the same time as the epigrams; on the contrary, it seems likely that the epigrams were written at Felpham before he returned to London. By the time he had settled in South Molton Street he had forgiven Hayley; in fact he was inclined to believe that much of the fault lay with himself. He was brought to this changed attitude by the fracas he had with the soldier Scolfield just as he was leaving Felpham. The soldier's deliberate perjury, in accusing him of sedition, shocked Blake profoundly, and he suddenly realized that there was a vast difference between an offence committed in ignorance and one committed by design. Hayley, he concluded, had offended him ignorantly, and his (Blake's) own passiveness only served to increase the offence. Hence Blake asserted that whereas it was still true that he had been 'much degraded & injuriously treated; but if it all arise from my own fault, I ought to blame myself'.[1] His conclusion was that all he had had to endure in the way of Hayley's lack of sympathy and interference 'is come from the spiritual World for Good, & not for Evil'.[1] So he asked Butts to burn 'what I have peevishly written about any friend'.[1] His changed attitude to Hayley was supported by the latter's sterling efforts in his defence. Moreover, in his first letter to Hayley after his return to London, announcing his safe arrival, he referred to himself as 'your devoted rebel'. If he could speak in this frank and good-humoured manner of his previous association with Hayley, we may be sure that the air had been cleared, that the epigrams were written at Felpham, and that Blake was not hypocritical.

It may of course be argued that to write epigrams at Felpham at the same time as keeping up polite conversation would have been equally hypocritical, but the circumstances were different. While at Felpham Blake tried to treat his employer and host with deference, and repressed the caustic retorts his fiery and independent spirit prompted him to make; but try as he could, and he made the effort for three years, he made no impression on Hayley, who read his works with 'contempt', and only when Blake took a more positive line did Hayley's ideas begin to change.

[1] *To Butts*, 16 Aug. 1803.

X

CONCLUSION

HAVING outlined the main doctrines that go to make up Blake's system of theology, we should now be in a position to define his religious position. Blake considered himself to be a follower of Christ. 'I profess myself a Christian,'[1] he said, and declared 'I must . . . do my endeavour to live to the Glory of our Lord & Saviour',[2] believing that his happiness was 'Secure in Jesus our Lord'.[3] After a careful consideration of his ideas, there seems no reason whatsoever why his claim should not be allowed.

To Blake the religion of Christ was a living reality which embraced the whole of existence, in particular 'Christianity is Art'.[4] This statement requires explication in order to understand Blake's conception of Christianity as a whole.

The contacts between religion and art are many and varied. Both of them come from within, from a divine motivation stirring man into activity; both of them are a motion of the soul, giving expression in thought and action to the spirit of life; both of them derive from man's awe at the mystery of being. Again, the two have the same object—the search for unity, for the rhythm of relationships—and the same desire to transfigure life and penetrate beyond the outward show. Both art and religion reveal truth: art under the aspect of beauty, Christianity in the light of the Incarnation which discloses the holiness of life. It was considerations such as these that led Blake to identify art and religion; but in arriving at this position he was influenced most strongly by his mysticism and his own individual artistic experience, for the artist and the mystic meet along the path of imagination. 'The Man who never in his Mind & Thoughts travel'd to Heaven Is No Artist,'[5] he affirmed, and 'I know of no other Christianity and of no other Gospel than the liberty both of body & mind to exercise the Divine Arts of Imagination'.[6]

To Blake, art was a religious activity; 'Prayer is the Study of Art. Praise is the Practice of Art. Fasting &c., all relate to

---

[1] Watson, pp. 4–5.
[2] *To Butts*, 25 Apr. 1803.
[3] *To Hayley*, 11 Dec. 1805.
[4] Laocoon.
[5] Reynolds, p. 56.
[6] *Jerusalem*, 77.

Art';[1] indeed 'Jesus & his Apostles & Disciples were all Artists'.[1] The best commentary on this last statement may be given in the words of Oscar Wilde: 'The very basis of his [Christ's] nature was the same as that of the nature of the artist—an intense and flamelike imagination. He realized in the entire sphere of human relations that imaginative sympathy which in the sphere of art is the sole secret of creation.' Similarly the ethics of Christianity are an art and not a code; 'in His actual teaching Christ speaks as if He conceived conduct as "the art of life" an art of solid building, yet with something of the dancer's gaiety. There is a kind of aesthetic quality about His approach to moral questions; one is always left with the feeling that His teaching is, as it were, "beyond morality". The word "morality" suggests rules, system, law, theoretical principle: but in the teaching of Christ there is always a sense of creation and adventure, a suggestion of buoyancy, paradox, *abandon*.'[2] With such thoughts in mind, Blake declared that 'the Mocker of Art is the Mocker of Jesus'.[3]

Christianity involves a creative attitude to life; man is called to co-operate with the Father in His work of creation; he is enabled to do this, despite his fall, because through Jesus Christ, the God-Man, his inner harmony has been restored and union with God has again become a possibility. Christianity is then the art of arts, and its mission is identical with that of the artist whose search for truth and beauty can lead him as certainly as the path of asceticism and moral endeavour to God who is the Crown of all. Christianity gives meaning and purpose to existence, revealing truth and beauty, and bringing Eternal Life to man, who henceforth enjoys the Divine Vision and is a member of the One Man, through continual acts of self-annihilation. 'The unproductive Man is not a Christian',[1] and Blake, whose fecundity of genius was outstanding, was surely a follower of Jesus.

'The strong Man', said Blake, in words which may be applied to himself, 'acts from conscious superiority, and marches on in fearless dependance on the divine decrees, raging with the inspiration of a prophet's mind.'[4] It is true that he had his 'intellectual peculiarity, that must be myself alone shut up in myself, or

---

[1] Laocoon. [2] B. H. Streeter in *Adventure*, 1930, p. 66.
[3] *To Hayley*, 11 Dec. 1805. [4] *Descriptive Catalogue*, v.

reduced to nothing',[1] and this deliberate severance from institutional religion was undoubtedly to the detriment not only of his art but also of his whole system of theology, since it rendered him too apt to over-emphasize those truths which he perceived, whilst neglecting other equally important aspects of the Gospel. His theology, as a consequence, lacks balance, his insights are partial, he is occasionally heterodox, and while he penetrated deeply into some doctrines, his appreciation of others was but slight. He did, however, grasp one vital factor, that if the religion of Christ is to mean anything at all, a man must make it his own by personal discovery; it is regrettable that in achieving this he did not seek more help from the wisdom of the Church. Blake was a Protestant, not a Catholic, and as such he had an inadequate conception of the nature of the Church which he repudiated.

Blake's use of dialectic, with its affirmation of thesis and antithesis, both equally true, obscures the development of his thought, since no idea is ever completely discarded but is incorporated into the whole. Yet some development there undoubtedly was: this is particularly evident in his ethic and in the closely associated problem of asceticism. His doctrine of the Fall reveals more elaboration than development, but his belief in providence, clearly expressed in the *Songs of Innocence*, suffered a temporary eclipse in the *Book of Urizen*, only to reassert itself with renewed vigour and certitude in the later works. His doctrine of God also reveals a similar evolution; the beneficent creator of the early poems is for a short time replaced by a 'very Cruel Being', only to reappear as one with the Divine Humanity who fashions the world as an act of mercy to provide a means for man to reascend to heaven. However, despite these several points, Blake's theology remained remarkably consistent, and such changes as it underwent were more the fruit of a deepening understanding of the divine mysteries than a process of conscious development involving the rejection of what had gone before.

Taking the Apostles' Creed as a basis, we may now summarize Blake's theology to the effect that he believed in 'God the Father ... Maker of Heaven and Earth: and in Jesus Christ his only Son our Lord, who was born ... of Mary, Suffered under

[1] *To Linnell*, Feb. 1827.

Pontius Pilate, Was Crucified, dead and buried, He descended into hell; The third day he rose again from the dead; he ascended into heaven and sitteth on the right hand of God the Father; from thence he shall come to judge both the quick and the dead . . . and in the Holy Ghost . . . the Communion of Saints, the forgiveness of sins . . . and life everlasting.' Although there are several significant omissions in this, we are bound to affirm that his doctrines fall within the general tradition of Christianity.

To those who have glorified Blake as the great heresiarch this conclusion may seem somewhat of an anti-climax, but to those whose experience of the Christian religion is as vital as was that of Blake, it is but a further testimony to the compelling truth of the Gospel for all those who approach it in a spirit of adventure and with a thirst for that wisdom 'that resteth in the heart of him that hath understanding'.

BIBLIOGRAPHY

A complete list of books by and about Blake will be found in *A Bibliography of William Blake*, by G. Keynes, 1921, and in *The Life of William Blake*, by A. Gilchrist, edited by Ruthven Todd, 1942. The following is a list of those books either quoted or referred to in the foregoing study:

1. STUDIES OF BLAKE

MAUNG BA-HAN, *William Blake. His Mysticism*, 1924.

H. BRUCE, *William Blake in this World*, 1925.

O. BURDETT, *William Blake*, 1926.

G. K. CHESTERTON, *William Blake* [1910].

FOSTER DAMON, *William Blake. His Philosophy and Symbols*, 1924.

T. S. ELIOT, *Selected Essays, 1917–1932*, 1932.

C. GARDNER, *Vision and Vesture*, 1929.

R. GARNETT, *William Blake. Poet and Painter*, 1895.

A. GILCHRIST, *Life of William Blake*, 1863. (Edited by Ruthven Todd, 1942.)

L. A. DUNCAN-JOHNSTONE, *A Psychological Study of William Blake*, 1945.

G. KEYNES, *A Bibliography of William Blake*, 1921.

—— *The Writings of William Blake*, 1925, 3 vols.

—— *Poetry and Prose of William Blake*, 1927.

M. R. LOWERY, *Windows of the Morning, A Critical Study of William Blake's Poetical Sketches*, 1783. Yale Studies in English, vol. xciii, 1940.

B. H. MALKIN, *A Father's Memoirs of His Child*, 1806. (Reprinted by Symons.)

J. MIDDLETON MURRY, *William Blake*, 1936.

Modern Language Review, xxxviii, 2 April 1943.

Morning Light, xxvi, 1903.

H. N. MORRIS, *Flaxman, Blake, Coleridge and Other Men of Genius influenced by Swedenborg*, 1915.

New Church Weekly, xl, 1917.

ALLARDYCE NICOLL, *William Blake and His Poetry*, 1922.

M. O. PERCIVAL, *William Blake's Circle of Destiny*, 1938.

The Quest, xi, 1919.

H. CRABB ROBINSON, *Diary, Letters and Reminiscences*. (Reprinted by Symons.)

W. M. ROSSETTI, *The Poetical Works of William Blake, with a Prefatory Memoir*, 1893.

D. SAURAT, *Blake and Modern Thought*, 1929.

—— *Blake and Milton*, 1935.

E. H. SHORT, *Blake*, 1925.

D. J. SLOSS AND J. P. R. WALLIS, *The Prophetic Writings of William Blake*, 2 vols., 1926.

J. T. SMITH, *Biographical Sketch of Blake*, 1825. (Reprinted by Symons.)

A. SYMONS, *William Blake*, 1907.

F. TATHAM, *Life of William Blake*, edited by A. G. B. Russell, 1906.

H. C. WHITE, *The Mysticism of William Blake*. University of Wisconsin Studies in Language and Literature, No. 23, 1927.

J. WICKSTEED, *Blake's Innocence and Experience*, 1928.
W. P. WITCUTT, *Blake, A Psychological Study*, 1946.

2. OTHER WORKS, THEOLOGICAL, HISTORICAL, ETC., REFERRED TO OR QUOTED

C. J. ABBEY AND J. H. OVERTON, *The English Church in the Eighteenth Century*, 1902.
K. BARTH, *The Word of God and the Word of Man*, 1928.
L. B. DE BEAUMONT, *Spiritual Reconstruction and the Religious Unrest of the Age*, 1918.
N. BERDYAEV, *Freedom and the Spirit*, 1935.
—— *The Destiny of Man*, 1937.
R. FRY, *Vision and Design*, 1920.
F. HARTMANN, *The Life and Doctrines of Jacob Boehme*, 1891.
E. HERMAN, *The Meaning and Value of Mysticism*, 1922.
R. HINDMARSH, *The Rise and Progress of the New Jerusalem Church*, 1861.
S. HOBHOUSE, *Selected Mystical Writings of William Law*, 1938.
L. HODGSON, *The Doctrine of the Trinity*, 1943.
SIR J. JEANS, *Physics and Philosophy*, 1943.
J. MARITAIN, *Questions de conscience*, Paris.
C. SMYTH, *The Art of Preaching, 747–1939*, 1940.
B. H. STREETER, *Adventure*, 1930.
SWEDENBORG, *Opera*.
E. UNDERHILL, *The Fruits of the Spirit*, 1942.
—— *Mysticism*, 14th edition, 1942.
G. VANN, *Of His Fullness*, 1941.
VON HÜGEL, *Eternal Life*, 1912.
N. P. WILLIAMS, *The Ideas of the Fall and of Original Sin*, 1927.

INDEX